When God is in the Whisper

Requests for information should be directed to:

Tara Browder Media

tarabrowdermedia@gmail.com

ISBN-13:978-1500771737

ISBN-10:150077132

Dedication

To My Parents—Thank you for teaching me how to walk in relationship with the God behind the whisper. Through choosing to leave your comfortable lives in America to be missionaries with your two children, you taught me that extravagant obedience to His voice is one of the greatest demonstrations of our love back to God.

Acknowledgments

Before I thank or acknowledge anyone, I want to give praise and honor to Daddy God for being a faithful Father who has never left me or forsaken me. Any amount of love I am able to express is because He first loved me. I am so thankful that He gives all of us the blessing of being a part of His divinely orchestrated plans for our lives and the lives of others. This book is about You and for You, Daddy God!

Mike and Debbie Legg: for your unceasing encouragement of me as your "daughter," believing in God's promises over my life even when I waivered during one of my darkest hours, and providing endless love, laughter, and wisdom.

Uncle Darrel and Aunt Sue: You have been a constant source of wisdom and encouragement. Through contending for God's restoration of all things lost in my life, you have stood with me and fought for me in the times of my greatest blessing and heartbreak. Thank you for being a source of consistent faith, strength, love and wisdom.

Grandpa and Grandma Masters: You have given me a heritage and legacy to follow God no matter what the cost and have taught by example that He is truly the Pearl of Great Price. Thank you for your love and unceasing prayers for me. This book represents a part of my destiny you prayed into existence.

Kay Duffield, Anne Smith, and Kathy Schroeder: For you friendship and your shared passion for the healing of people body, mind and spirit. Your prayers and friendship have been a joy and healing balm to my heart many times over! I love you all dearly!

Meredith Brown, Kathryn Fitzhugh, Anne and Bill Smith, Kathy and Mickey Schroeder, Chuck and Kay Duffield, Sarah and Ledio Ago, Annette and Gene Scheel, Kelly Roberson, Elise Jackson, Mike and Debbie Legg, Terry and Connie Smith, Jothi and Johnny Clinton, the McNichols Family, Heather Carmen, Lori and Bryan Pugh, Tom and Vicky Eckhardt, Meg Russell, Vicki McLucas, Linda Ross, Susan and Keith Mongeau, Emily Galloway, Kayci Lewis, Dana Wallace, Nathan Johns, Erin Simms, Jonathan Seiver, the Haddocks and the Andrades: You have been those who have run the race alongside me throughout key moments of my entire spiritual journey. You have all been ones who have rejoiced with me when I have rejoiced and grieved with me when I have grieved. You are gifts from God to me, and I cherish your friendship.

Michelle, Dave, and Dylan Haddock: for being a family to me in one of my darkest hours. You all have known Gethsemane, but you have also known resurrection. Without the prayers, compassion, love, and joy that I received in your home, this book would not have happened. Also, I am forever grateful for the donation of your time and resources to get this gal into the 21st century with her website, media, and ministry workshops.

Jonathan Seiver: for being an unwavering brother and friend and for your countless hours of listening to me read the manuscript for this book as you imparted Godly wisdom related to the content therein.

April Chang and Meg Russell: for donating your precious time and skills to endlessly edit and re-edit the manuscript for this book.

Cameron Goodman: for donating your time and graphic design skills to make the cover of this book a reality.

Amber and Sergio Andrade: for being my family in Texas and providing a laughter and love filled home and lots of dance breaks and family dinners in between sessions of writing for this project.

Nathan and Ashley Johns and Nathan Johns Photography of Austin, TX: for permitting me to use your photography art for the book cover, assisting in the creation of the cover, and taking my headshots. You have gone above and beyond to artistically represent the words of this book.

Ramy Antoun and the ministry of Rev 1211: for encouraging me and many others to overcome by the word of our testimony.

Table of Contents

Part Two: How to Begin Your Journey

Foreword

In the church today, there is a common struggle among many believers, as we hear and see powerful acts of God being done by the few, but not the many, including us! We wonder why the same Spirit in us isn't producing similar results. We love Jesus. We have His Spirit. We eagerly pursue His gifts. For some reason however, we don't see in us what we see in them, and we may become discouraged and fearful to step out and end up wondering if we will ever hear His voice.

When God is in the Whisper is an accessibility ramp for today's followers of Jesus, making it possible to gain access to the place we have longed to be. What Tara Browder has set out to do, and has wonderfully accomplished, is to build a ramp over the obstacles that cause fear and paralysis and therefore a discouraged spirit. In the pages you are about to read, you will find a renewed hope for how God is going to begin using you in ways you never thought possible.

As you read Tara's account of how the Lord taught her to take baby steps, then to walk, then to stumble, and then finally to run, you will be refreshed at how honest, vulnerable, and real Tara is. Tara is today as she has always been, simply a servant who dared to acknowledge the whispers of God and begin following them. Her joy without agenda, her heart's desire to make the power of God accessible to all, and her ability to stay grounded in simplicity as "one of us" has never failed to impart a refreshing spirit to those she ministers to. Without trying to impress you, she will simply give you access to what the Lord did with her. Then you will begin to see how the Lord can also do that with you. That is the seed planting. After you are firmly established in the place of hope and confidence, Tara will then, in the latter part of the book, set down easy to follow steps on how to cultivate the gift of God within you. Finally, there is the unwritten third part, which is yours to write, as you begin to hear the whispers of God and follow them in what will be the harvest that brings Jesus glory and you joy.

Listen as you read! You may begin to hear something faint, like someone very wonderful and loving and kind whispering something special to your heart even before you finish the book. This will be the beginning of what will be a life-long adventure of discovering what it means to say, "*When God is in the Whisper*".

Tom Eckhardt

Pastor, Bradley Epworth Church

Peoria, Illinois

Introduction

It's best to start off this book by explaining what it is not before explaining what it is. This book is not a collection of "blow-your-socks-off" kinds of stories of radical obedience that no real person could actually put into practice in their everyday life. It's not a collection of "show-off" examples that could not be executed by the everyday stay-at-home mom or dad, teacher, pastor, or retiree. It's not for only the young or only the mature. It's not just for the perfect or the seasoned follower of Christ.

When God is in the Whisper is a collection of stories of obedience to God's still, and often times, more-quiet-than-we-would-like, voice. These stories come from the life of a child of God and everyday average believer who has stumbled upon, and many times stumbled through, opportunities to adventure with God in childlike obedience, and, as a result has witnessed God's amazing love and supernatural power released in her life and in the lives of others.

This book is a challenge and a call to draw you into your own journey of not only recognizing God's whispers but also responding to them in childlike obedience. I pray that what lies on the other side of reading the book are adventures with God beyond your wildest imaginations as you and others in your spheres of influence encounter the love and power of God released through obedience to His whispers.

Part One:

The Story of My Journey

Chapter One

A Date with Destiny

It was spring of 2001, and I had just relocated from Kansas City, Missouri to Charlotte, North Carolina. I had asked God for a date, but what I really needed was a job. Perhaps my odd request could be chalked up to the fact that my stressed-out self had just trudged from interview to interview for a month. These interviews resulted in me gaining lots of experience ironing the one suit I owned for such occasions, but failed to result in employment. Even though the steam setting on my iron was working smashingly well, my steam for job hunting was depleted.

I was shocked by my own request for a date instead of a job. Not fully aware of my motives behind such a prayer, I expected no response from God, much less an answer. After all, I had asked Him for what I wanted instead of what I needed. I assumed God was not to be busied with my frivolous wants. Unless I selflessly prayed for things that really mattered, I could expect to leave a message on His voicemail, but a return call from Him was highly unlikely. As a result, full of self-pity, I placed my seemingly presumptuous and selfish prayer for a date into a file labeled "God's Too Busy for These Prayers" in my heart.

After tucking my prayer away into the abyss of forgotten requests, I returned to my normal worrying. How does one react after a month without pay as bills begin to roll in? Desperate times call for desperate measures. I was plagued with thoughts of why God would prompt me to move halfway across the country to a city where I would end up jobless. So, I decided to take a job that my college educated self-assumed she had forever dodged...cleaning.

A friend of mine owned a cleaning business, and being a kind soul who cared about my financial situation, she offered me a part time job cleaning houses. My job title in my mind, "Head Toilet Cleaner", unfortunately wasn't going to be the resume' booster I was searching for, but, fortunately, this job at least paid the bills.

After spending a week or two cleaning toilets and wiping up hair from people's bathroom sinks, I woke up on a Saturday morning wondering where God was and when He was going to provide me a job that I actually enjoyed. My friend whistled while she worked. Apparently she thrived in her element of meticulously cleaning; however, this cleaning job was not my cup of tea.

I was in the bathroom—the place where God seems to speak to many people. It is one of the few places we actually sit down long enough for God to get our attention. As I was preparing for my usual Saturday, I heard Him whisper. He interrupted my regularly scheduled program of complaining about my job search to give me an important news bulletin. I'd love to say that I heard the sound of God's booming voice the likes of which was heard by Moses on Mt. Sinai[1], but it came so quickly and so quietly. In fact, it wasn't really a voice at all. On that Saturday, while I was prepping for my mundane day and complaining about being promoted to "Head Toilet Cleaner", the whisper came in the form of a *thought*. Yes, a *thought*. And the thought was:

We are going on that date today.

Once that sentence bumped up against my intellect, I began to wonder about several things. I first thought that this was surely not God speaking. I had forgotten my request for a date after putting it in the "God's Too Busy for These Prayers" file, and I was so surprised that He remembered it. Second, I considered the possibility that in the depths of my subconscious, I may not have forgotten about my request for a date, and I was simply having a thought that was "just me" and not God's idea. In the middle of all my doubts, a small part of me--probably the childlike part of me-- entertained the idea that there was a small chance that this could be God whispering to me.

---

1 Exodus 19:16-19

As I finished getting ready for the day, I wondered how I should respond if this thought was actually a whisper from God. I figured it would require some sort of action on my part. But honestly, I struggled with determining the strategy to get the ball rolling for this date. After all, it had been years since I had even been on a date. Regardless of that, I had another file tucked away in my heart labeled "Awesome Date Ideas for Whenever the Curse of Singlehood is Broken in My Life." Despite my rusty skills in the dating arena, this file contained my thoughts on the perfect date, which I believed must include dressing up and sharing a meal with the man I loved.

Was it really that simple? If God was actually whispering, was I only required to get dressed up and pick a restaurant? That seemed easy enough. After all, what did I have to lose? With the realization that not much risk was involved with this blind faith date, I started preparing for my date with Jesus.

As was putting the final touches on my make-up, I decided where I wanted to have lunch on this date. So you ask: How does one go about selecting a restaurant for their first official date with God? Now, I figured if the richest man in the universe invited me on a date, He was most likely not planning on us going "dutch." If Jesus didn't plan on paying, based on my financial portfolio at the time, we would have been picnicking over a bowl of Ramen noodles and peanut butter sandwiches.

Knowing that He was paying set me free to select a place I had spied as the place to go when I got my first real pay check. It was one of those places my Southern friends would call a "Soul-Food Hole-in-the-Wall" where one's elbows stick to the sweet tea lacquered vinyl table cloth and where one savors the best fried chicken, corned bread, and collard greens in town. Wow! At this point, obedience to God's still small voice was super easy! I was salivating, dressed to the nines, and ready to head out on the town.

Now, I would love to say that I was completely confident Jesus intended to pay for this date, but my faith, was small, about the size of a mustard seed[2] to be exact. At that time, my little mustard seed faith provided me a peace knowing that if Jesus stood me up, VISA would rescue me, so, armed with my little faith and my credit card, I headed out the door.

I arrived at the restaurant that my jobless self couldn't really afford, sat down in the booth and ordered everything my little heart desired--from sweet tea to a Southerner's favorite dessert, banana pudding. I savored each and every bite, but when the bill arrived, buyer's remorse hovered over me like the Grim Reaper.

While I was kicking myself for ordering a sweet tea instead of water, which would have been free, I noticed a woman sitting at a table across the restaurant. After finishing her meal, she came over

---

2 Luke 17:6, Matt 17:20

to my table. Smiling from ear to ear, she asked me if had enjoyed my meal. A foodie at heart, I explained to her what I enjoyed about each course. Afterwards she delightedly revealed that she co-owned the restaurant. Without skipping a beat, she shared how she had been watching me as I enjoyed her mom's fried chicken. After asking me if I knew Jesus, she told me that He brought me to the city of Charlotte for a reason.

I couldn't believe it. I drove to a restaurant where I had never dined before, and God gave someone a prophetic word for me while I was eating. I was beginning to consider the possibility that this really was an actual date with Him until the woman told me I could settle my check whenever I was ready.

I slowly gathered my belongings and made my way to the cash register to pay. At this point, I decided that God had, in fact, stood me up, or I had failed in hearing His voice. So, I pulled out my VISA. As the owner rang up each item I ordered into the cash register, my face remained calm, collected, and friendly. Yet, on the inside, I was cringing as I awaited the grand total of my gluttony. Then, she hit the total button, and the blue neon price indicator sparkled "$0.00". Through her cheerful grin, she sweetly said, "This meal is on the Lord today!"

Of all the things she could have said, she told me Jesus was paying! She could have said, "Welcome to Charlotte! This meal is on the house" or "This meal is on us today." Nope. She didn't say those things because this was my date with Jesus and it was on Him, not on anyone else.

Now, I know what you are probably thinking at this point. *Did you actually just get a date or did you eventually get a job?* Let me put you at ease. The same God who swept me off of my feet on our date made certain I obtained employment, and I never missed paying one bill.

Now that we got that looming question answered, perhaps you are still thinking:

> *How do you know this date wasn't just a coincidence? Even if this wasn't just a coincidence, what if people responded to every single one of their thoughts as if they were from God? That sounds dangerous!*

> *What about the big decisions in life that may be costly to not just you but others? Does this childlike faith apply in those situations?*

> *Does God expect everyone to live like this? I am not sure I am game for that kind of risk.*

> *What if you do step out and follow these "God whispers" and it doesn't work out or worse.... it's an epic fail?*

If you'll stick with me, answers to these questions and more will unfold as I share my life's journey on when God has been in the whisper. In part one of this book, through reading my personal testimonies of listening to and obeying God's voice, I pray God will stir you to pursue His whispers in your own life, and as you read part two, my prayer is that you will receive practical ways to apply action to your childlike faith in His voice. Most importantly, my prayer is that through this entire book, you not only grasp in a greater way, the reality of God's whispers in your life, but the love of the One behind the whispers.

Chapter Two

Deer Legs and Watermelon Seeds

Have you ever seen those deer heads hanging on the wall at backwoods restaurants or in the home of an avid hunter? As a child, these trophies piqued my curiosity. My father, a man who always possessed the ability to make me laugh, used to tell me that the rest of the deer's body and legs were on the other side of the wall. He told me that people cut holes in the wall so a live deer could walk up and stick its head in it. With childlike innocence and trust, I believed my dad. I believed him so much that until I learned he was only just joking, I would actually check to see if the rest of the deer was on the other side of the wall.

My dad also "lied" about watermelon seeds. Who, at some point in childhood wasn't told that when they swallow watermelon seeds, a watermelon would grow in their stomach? Maybe that just happened to me, but once again, when my father told me myths like this, my trust and belief in what he said were never disconnected from my action. Whenever I ate watermelon, I cautiously navigated around those little black seeds, and quickly spit them out if they managed to slip past the security checkpoints I had in place. I never wanted to discover what it was like to have to have a watermelon surgically removed, so I circumnavigated those seeds--no questions asked.

These examples may seem a little silly, but when I consider what my trust in my earthly father's words looked like, I wonder if Jesus was talking about this kind of trust in Mark 10:15 when He said, "Truly, I say to you, whoever does not receive the kingdom of God like a child shall not enter it." This describes the faith it requires to accept Christ as our Savior. I knew I possessed enough trust and faith to make a choice to become a follower of Christ. Could that same trust be applied to hearing and responding to His voice even when that voice is not loud—maybe merely a whisper?

This kind of whisper is described in the story of Elijah on Mount Horeb in 1 Kings 19:9-13:

> There he came to a cave and lodged in it. And behold, the word of the Lord came to him, and he said to him, "What are you doing here, Elijah?" He said, "I have been very jealous for the Lord, the God of hosts. For the people of Israel have forsaken your covenant, thrown down your altars, and killed your prophets with the sword, and I, even I only, am left, and they seek my life, to take it away." And he said, "Go out and stand on the mount before the Lord."

And behold, the Lord passed by, and a great and strong wind tore the mountains and broke in pieces the rocks before the Lord, but the Lord was not in the wind. And after the wind an earthquake, but the Lord was not in the earthquake. And after the earthquake a fire, but the Lord was not in the fire. And after the fire the sound of a low **whisper**. And when Elijah heard it, he wrapped his face in his cloak and went out and stood at the entrance of the cave. And behold, there came a voice to him and said, "What are you doing here, Elijah?"

In this scene, Elijah fled Jezebel and ascended to the same mountaintop where Moses heard God's voice in the fire of the burning bush. However, in this circumstance, God wasn't in the fire. He wasn't in the wind or the earthquake either. His voice would not be found in the loud pomp and circumstance as it was in the case of Moses. If Elijah relied on solely what Moses had experienced, he would have been searching for God's voice in all the wrong places, and would have failed to recognize God's whisper or still small voice[3].

How many times do we wait for and even demand the fire, wind, or earthquake of His voice before we even begin to step towards something we think God might be speaking? Are we so

---

3 From 1 Kings 19:12 (King James Version of the Holy Bible)

accustomed to the glitz and glamour of immediate gratification in our society that God's still small voice and whisper have become outdated or obsolete to us? Have we traded in our need for His personal whisper in exchange for podcasts and inspirational quotes people post on Facebook? Have we failed to realize that our deepest relationship and wildest adventures in God will come from something as organic as His whisper? No bells. No whistles. No fire. No wind. Just Him and His quiet voice.

After that date with Jesus in 2001, I realized that at some point in my life, I had unlearned how to trust God in this childlike, simple way. I cherished the whispers He shared with me in the times when no one else was around and when we talked as friends. That date was a whisper only He and I knew about, and that made it a special moment between me and God that could never be obtained from living off of someone else's journey or "burning bush"[4] experience.

What had happened on that date invited me to become childlike in my faith again. Acting as a catalyst for change, that date challenged me to marry faith and action just like the moments I checked for deer legs behind the wall or spit watermelon seeds into the backyard

---

4 Moses also had an encounter with God on Mt. Horeb in Exodus 3:1-2 (the same place Elijah encountered God) In his case, God spoke through a burning bush of fire, but in Elijah's case God spoke in a whisper. God will not necessarily give us the same encounters as others. We must look for Him in the form He reveals to us.

My journey in embracing this newly discovered faith began with an analysis of when and how I had unlearned how to trust God like a child. After allowing God to do a little exploring and searching of my heart, He revealed to me that human logic had something to do with the loss of my childlike trust. When human logic and reason become our only teachers, we run into trouble. That trouble is the result of only allowing faith and God's wisdom to step in as substitutes when logic and reason take a day off. When this happens, we lose our childlike innocence to chase after dreams, and we shrink back from stepping into a realm of God's provision that exceeds anything we could ask for or imagine.

If Peter's only teachers were logic and reason, would he have walked on water?[5] Did logic convince Noah to build the ark?[6] Did reason inspire Abraham to take Isaac up Mount Moriah?[7] Would Joseph have trusted that he would be remembered in prison if he had relied solely on his own reasoning?[8] I could pose the same questions related to so many others in scripture. God clearly works outside the neat little boxes we place Him in, and that date in 2001 challenged me to not only let Him out of the box but set

---

5 Matthew 14:22-33

6 Genesis 6:11-7:5

7 Genesis 22:1-14

8 Genesis 39-40

myself free from my own box as well. It sent me on an ongoing hunt for treasures in the every day mundane.

These were the small beginnings of my journey in listening to and responding to God's whispers. As a result of this process, I began to see God do the miraculous in my life and the lives of others. After only a little time committing to live with this kind of childlike trust, I was hooked. I was ruined to live my life in any other way. Was it costly to start living this way? Yes. Was it worth it? A hundred times...yes! Have I always gotten it right? No. However, I have learned that it's much better to live in the adventure of responding to what we guess God might be saying than have no response at all. The stories you are about to read reveal this reality.

Chapter Three

Was that Just a Coincidence?

What if the things that we label as random coincidences in life are divine appointments from God? This concept was put to the test in August 2010 on the day my friend Tamela Ryan and I got lost on the streets of Harrisburg, Pennsylvania. The day seemed like it couldn't have been more complete, but God upstaged all of our plans with one of His. With bellies full of jumbo sea scallops and eyes satisfied with the beautiful view of the Susquehanna River running through the city, Tamela and I had decided to continue in our much needed girls-day-out and headed to the car chatting away, as always.

In my world, talking and driving don't always mix. When I start talking to or intently listening to a friend on a road trip, if I'm not careful, I'll find myself driving 40 mph in a 50 mph zone (I drive slower when I am talking), or in this case, missing my turn. Thankfully, I had my GPS, and my beloved Australian man guiding me back on course. His demand to "recalculate" through the GPS speaker shocked me back into reality, and I searched for a place to make a U-turn.

We were lost, but not for long. I made a sharp left when I could, and we ended up on a street that reminded me of Sesame Street -- little brownstone houses with steps out front; kids jumping rope on the sidewalk; parents sitting on their porches sipping out of brightly colored plastic cups. The scene was an iconic picture of what a family weekend used to be in the 1980s—a time when the street lights turning on was the sign to come home for dinner. My attention was drawn toward a little girl walking on the sidewalk in front of her family home. She appeared to be wearing clothes designed for a woman her mother's age because they didn't make kid's clothes in her size. Not only did she wear women's sized clothing, but she also walked like a woman burdened with the sufferings of life. She already had a story, and she seemed to be only nine or ten years old.

In the ten seconds it took to pass her, my heart was undone. I had another one of these God whispers, and this time it came in the form of a picture in my mind. A snapshot of a teenage girl bullied at school flashed through my mind. It was a lightning bolt designed to get my attention--a storm was on the horizon if the winds didn't shift. After this, His whisper came in a different form; this time it was an impression in my heart. I sensed that if God didn't intersect her life, she would never know her purpose or worth. All this happened because I made a wrong turn and had to recalculate.

Now, I don't have this response every time I pass by a kid on the more chubby side, but I had learned since that date with Jesus in 2001 that if I have an impression like that come into my heart, the wise thing to do is to respond in some way even if the response is just a quick prayer.

Compassion for her welled up within me. I, too, was one of those kids with leftover baby fat in school. I empathize with their struggle, and so does God. For some reason, in addition to the picture God planted in my heart and mind, He wanted me to feel her emotional pain. I had to see and feel what this young girl would experience if things didn't change in her life. Because I had learned over the nine years since my date with Jesus in 2001 that God was often gave me opportunities to partner with Him through these possible God thoughts, I started to pray for the little girl. My friend Tamela joined me in our little moment of intercession as the Australian man in the GPS took care of getting us back on track to our next destination.

In my prayer, I specifically asked God to send her people to intersect her life and love her the way He does. After a few moments of prayer, unaware that it was not a mere coincidence that we had gotten lost, Tamela and I went about our day.

It was six or seven hours since we prayed in the car for the little girl on "Sesame Street." Attending a church service, sharing some diner eats, and purchasing the movie tickets had all happened right on schedule. As Tamela purchased some popcorn, I decided to use the ladies' room before the movie. Little did I know, but I was about to happen upon what seemed at first to be a "coincidence." Upon entering the ladies' room, I was astounded at who I saw. At the sink washing her hands, was the little girl I had seen six or seven hours earlier in a neighborhood that was a fifteen-minute drive from where I now stood.

Clearly recognizing at this point that I was no longer part of a coincidence but part of a strategically arranged God plan that started hours before, I jumped in one of the stalls not knowing what to do next. Once again, I was getting ready to hear God speak to me in a bathroom just like He did in 2001 before my date.

Two things were very clear to me in that bathroom stall. Number One: Six hours prior, God had invited Tamela and I to "turn aside" like Moses did with the burning bush, hear Him speak about a little girl, and prompt us to pray for her. Number Two: Also like the story of Moses at the burning bush, I had no idea what to do in order to see God's purposes come to pass, and I felt completely unprepared and inadequate for the task.

I asked God what was going on, and He promptly said, "Well, you asked me to intersect her life with someone who can love her like I do." I nervously whispered to God, "Well, I didn't expect that person to be me. What do you want me to do?" He said, "Tell her that she is one of the most beautiful young ladies that you have ever seen." My first thought was "How am I going to tell her that without looking like a weirdo approaching a child in a movie theatre bathroom?" so I watched her go out the door and said nothing.

However, because I recognized that this couldn't just be a coincidence, I also knew that I had to obey God. I was desperately trying to think of how I could obey Him in a way that wasn't going to be weird. I asked for His wisdom as I rushed out the door to find her, and the words came to me as I saw her rejoin her grandmother. I decided to announce God's words of affirmation over her in the presence of her family. I walked over to them, and asked the grandmother if this young girl was her granddaughter. She said, "Yes," and as I opened my mouth to say something, the words came. I shared these words: "You should be so proud of your granddaughter. She is one of the most beautiful and polite young ladies I have ever seen. I just thought that she and you should know this". Without hesitation, the sad countenance I witnessed on the little girl's face earlier was transformed into a huge grin and her grandmother glowed with joy and pride. With a "Have a good night!" I was on my way into the theater.

As I walked to my seat, I heard the Lord say, "The enemy has plans for people, but you have the power to intersect people's lives with My plan and My love. That one sentence you proclaimed over that young girl's life reversed the collision course she was on with the enemy's plan."

I will probably not know until heaven if I really heard God's voice that day. However, something tells me that the same God who had me pray a prayer of compassion for that little girl knew I would see her again to put that prayer into action. Maybe He figured that based on our date in 2001 and other simple acts of responding to His whispers up until this encounter in 2010, I just might have the guts to obey Him.

Imagine if we, having Christ, who is the Hope of Glory[9], in us allowed ourselves to be that "intersection" where people could meet the Father. What if the circumstances that we write off as "accidents" and "coincidences" were treated with more tender care? Many times, His voice is so still and small that we fail to listen, but God invites us to be a people who don't require Him to yell if He wants to be heard and obeyed.

---

9 Colossians 1:27

Chapter Four

Living in the Moment

Many times we won't know if something is a whisper from God or just one of our random thoughts until we take initiative by stepping towards obeying those whispers. Sometimes that act of obedience is required right at the moment God speaks. Moses, a father in our faith, obeyed God even though he struggled with uncertainty about his call to be the deliverer of Israel in Egypt. He asked God how he would know if what he was hearing at the burning bush was true. God said in Exodus 3:12: "But I will be with you, and this shall be the sign for you, that I have sent you: *when* you have brought the people out of Egypt, you shall serve God on this mountain." It's interesting that God wasn't more specific here. He asked Moses to take Him at His word and obey before he saw signs or results.

God talking through a burning bush compelled Moses to obey. He didn't roll out the line-by -line specifics of how everything would take place. He didn't say "Only *after* you go before Pharaoh to request for freedom for My people ten times and get rejected the first nine times, watch Me release ten plagues on Egypt, and run for your life from a chariot led army into a dead end of the Red Sea will you know that what I am saying is true." I almost wonder if His saying these details would have stirred more fear in Moses than just leaving everything ambiguous. Regardless of God's motives for keeping the details of the journey top secret, He asked Moses to follow His voice and trust Him because of his pivotal encounter with God at the burning bush.

On the day I went on the date or the day I reached out to the little girl in the movie theater in Pennsylvania, I had far less at stake than Moses did, but it still required belief connected with action. Just like Moses, I didn't realize it was God until I obeyed. Little did I know at the time, but these were steps to greater journeys in God and greater testimonies of His love and power that waited for me around the corner. One of these came the night God whispered about buying my friend Nancy some flowers.

On a cold and rainy day in December 2011 in Mechanicsburg, Pennsylvania, I raced through the parking lot to get into the condo. It was not the kind of night I wanted to be out and about, especially since, I had just arrived home after a long day. I made my way up the steps to my room, and relished in the fact that none of my roommates had made it home yet. Although I loved them, I savored any precious moments of alone time I could find in our tight quarters. I was dreaming about sinking under my down comforter with a good book. As I started to relax and make my way to my closet to find some flannel pajamas, this thought flashed through my mind---*It's close to the anniversary of Nancy (one of my housemates) losing her husband to cancer a few years ago. Go get her some flowers and a card from Jesus.* Then, I thought of the story of how Jesus wept when Mary was grieving over Lazarus' death.

It literally only took ten seconds for that God whisper to pass through my mind, and five seconds to dismiss it as being "just me." It was drizzling outside. I was tired. I had a moment alone at the house. This mounting evidence "proved" to me that what I initially thought was God's voice telling me to get Nancy flowers was clearly "just me." However, those thoughts sounded like that all to familiar whisper that I had gotten to know really well over the years, and they refused to leave. They persistently pursued me like a dog nudging to be fed, and eventually, I listened. I couldn't figure out why these thoughts were accompanied by such urgency; however, I knew if I had just been presented with God's agenda for the night, those blueprints promised to offer more adventure and excitement than any book could ever provide.

Instead of wrapping myself into my down comforter, I put my winter coat back on and rushed out to get flowers and a card for Nancy from Jesus. I arrived at the grocery store, and another thought came---*"red roses."* This went against my inclination to purchase Gerbera daisies, which is what I would have preferred to receive as a gift, but I figured if the other thoughts were God speaking to me, then I would go with the flow and assume that this was Him too. I bought a bouquet of twelve red roses as well as a card, and I raced home to write in the card before Nancy got there.

Staying with the theme of the night, I included the analogy of Jesus weeping when Mary grieved, and I told Nancy in her card that Jesus was weeping with her. I placed the flowers and card in her room and waited for her to come home. One-hour prior, I was excited about being home alone, and now I found myself listening to every noise, hoping it was Nancy's car door signaling her arrival.

Finally, she got home, and for one hour she never noticed the flowers or the card in her room. A sucker for surprising people, I couldn't handle the suspense anymore. I thought that if I had to wait for her to notice the flowers, I was at least going to have some fun. I yelled to her in her room, "Hey, Nancy! What's your favorite flower?" And she promptly replied, "Red roses. Why?" My heart pounded with delight, and I thought I just might have heard God after all. She explained to me that her husband always gave her red roses and that God had often referred to her as His rose. She also shared that her sons had sent her roses since her husband passed away and that she would remove one rose from the dozen and leave it on her husband's grave, leaving her to enjoy the leftover eleven.

After hearing her sweet story, I couldn't stand the wait anymore. I stepped over to her room and told her to turn around to see what she had been missing for the last hour. She gasped with joy at the sight of what she had just described as her most prized gift from her husband, sons, and even God Himself. I left her to read her card in privacy. In just a few minutes she came into my room weeping. She said, "Did I tell you what God told me in the weeks after my husband died?" I knew that she had not shared this information with me. She then began relaying how she knew God was present with her when her husband passed away, but she often wondered what God was doing in that moment. I am sure that is often a question God is asked in times like that.

When she presented this question to God, He gave her a scripture reference--John 11:35, and when she looked it up, the words "Jesus wept" leapt off the page. In essence, He was telling her that He was not only with her, but that He was grieving with her and for her. After she revealed this, it made total sense why God whispered the story of Lazarus and Mary to me hours earlier when I went to the store to purchase her gift.

Overjoyed at how God had spoken to each of us, we both thought God had truly outdone Himself that night...that was, until Nancy counted the roses. She returned to her room, and not long after, I heard a loud scream. I rushed into her room and through her tears she exclaimed, "There are only eleven roses here!!!" God had pulled out all the stops for Nancy that night. Not only did He get her roses, but also He made sure one was taken out for her husband.

It was only after I had obeyed and *when* Nancy and I got to experience God and praise Him together for His love that night that I received the same revelation that Moses did after crossing the Red Sea. I now understood that our obedience may be required when we don't know all the details, but when we yield to God's voice even in the ambiguity, the outcome always leads to experiential knowledge of His glory, love, and power.

This reality is revealed in Proverbs 25:2 which aptly states, "It's the glory of God to conceal things, but the glory of kings is to search things out." In other words, it's a blessing for us to discover what God hides. He hides in ways that we can find Him if we are deliberate about our obedience and search for Him.

Earlier in the evening before I went shopping for flowers, not only the thoughts but also the sense of urgency to obey Him right at that moment were, in fact, God speaking to me. God didn't give me a reason for going out into the cold rain rather than waiting for a better moment to obey. However, if God being specific determined my obedience, I would have missed out on the treasure only those who seek Him, even in the ambiguity, find. Only He could have known that the florist at the grocery store made a mistake that very night and that there was a bouquet of eleven red roses, just short of a proper dozen, with Nancy's name on them.

Chapter Five

When Obeying Becomes Risky

Just a year before giving Nancy those flowers, I made a decision that cost a great deal more than that bouquet. This step of my journey to be someone who not only hears God's whispers but also obeys them got "very real," and, once again His whisper came in the form of a thought. This time, the thought was birthed from a seed of desire He placed in me as I was studying the scripture.

For a while, a divine agitation had been developing in me because I read scripture and didn't see the concepts that I was reading about manifest in my own life. I read verses like Mark 16:17-20, and I knew something was missing from my walk with God. It reads as follows:

> And these signs will accompany those who believe:
> in my name they will cast out demons; they will
> speak in new tongues; they will pick up serpents
> with their hands; and if they drink deadly poison, it
> will not hurt them; they will lay their hands on the
> sick, and they will recover.

When I read sections of scripture like this, I would wonder why I wasn't seeing these types of signs "follow" me. I really didn't care about drinking poison or picking up snakes, but I sure wanted to see God heal people when I prayed for them. One thing kept me from praying for people, though. My greatest obstacle to seeing the miraculous power of Jesus flow through me to others was my fear of not being able to explain to them why Jesus didn't heal them when I prayed.

My level of faith was nonexistent when it came to God healing people through me. I imagined myself stepping out to pray for people, them not getting healed, me awkwardly explaining why Jesus stood us up. My entire life I just decided that special people who were "gifted" in this existed for a reason, and, as a result, I abdicated any responsibility to honor what Jesus called all of us to do in Mark 16:20. Because of my fears, I decided to leave the praying for healing to the "experts," and I would just stick to prophesying or teaching. Even though scripture clearly revealed I could pray for the sick and see them healed if I believed in Jesus, I dug in my heels and chose to stay in my powerless status quo.

My status quo remained uninterrupted until God started planting ideas in my head about going to a ministry school that taught about things like praying for people's healing. For a while, I kept ignoring those thoughts because I knew obeying them would cost a lot more than a bouquet of flowers or gas to drive during my date with Jesus.

First of all, obedience to this "whisper" would cost me quitting a job that I loved. As a high school English teacher, I would be leaving behind students that I truly loved and cared for. I valued seeing them grow. I would miss my tenth graders dancing at their junior prom and growing into seniors applying for college and pursuing their dreams. The mama in me was heartbroken about this.

Second, responding to God's voice to go to ministry school would require me to leave a well paying job in a school that teachers would give anything to be able to work at. I was all too aware of how blessed I was to teach at Stone Bridge High School in Ashburn, VA. Prior to acquiring this teaching position, I mainly taught in inner city schools where I struggled daily to maintain the mental, physical, and spiritual stamina to educate tomorrow's leaders, and, unfortunately in some cases, tomorrow's prisoners. In those urban schools, not a week went by that some sort of altercation occurred between students in my classroom.

When I was hired at Stone Bridge, a school in suburbia, and a far cry different than any school where I had ever taught, a colleague of mine gave me the grand tour of the building and showed me my classroom. During the tour, I asked her a very important question that in my previous schools, I needed to obtain the answer to before the first day of school. I asked her how to call security when an emergency situation arose in my room. She laughed at me and asked, "What do you mean 'call security'? What kind of crazy school did you teach at before here? When a student misbehaves here, just tell them to go to the office to meet with the principal." I joined in her laughter at this point and said, "When you tell students to go to the office, they go? They actually do what you say without question?" At this moment, I realized I had been in the trenches of inner city education for so long that in some ways, I had just been surviving. That's why this new teaching position was like precious gold to me, and I thrived there.

At Stone Bridge High School, no student ever cussed me out and no one set fire to the bathroom trash cans. There, my students faithfully reported to class, had above average reading levels, and actually liked school. Parents volunteered to help me during their free time, and there was standing room only on parent night. I was in teacher heaven, and if I left this position to obey God, there would be no shortage of teachers lined up for my job.

Last but not least, yielding to God in this moment would require me to trust that God would provide financially as I raised support to attend this ministry school and launch into a part –time itinerant ministry circuit and missionary work overseas. I would be letting go of the highest salary I had ever earned. Going to this school would launch me into the unknown where a regular paycheck would be a thing of the past, and trusting God for provision even until the last minute would become the norm.

I didn't know if I was ready for this challenge. I possessed enough experiences with God's whispers to know that when He authored them, His provision to enable them to happen quickly followed. However, this whisper really upped the ante. If I was wrong and I had failed to hear God, the risk would come at a great expense to me; but I knew if I had heard God, I had much to gain.

After much prayer and seeking the counsel of close friends, family, and pastors, I chose to put in my notice and let the principal of my school know that I would not be returning the following year. I grieved over leaving. It was bittersweet for me, but soon, sweetness would overcome any of the pain in that sacrifice.

David said in 2 Samuel 24:24, "...I will not offer burnt offerings to the LORD my God that cost me nothing." As I packed my car and headed to Pennsylvania for school, I began to identify with this kind of sacrifice. Part of the sacrifice lay in the fact that in addition to relinquishing a job I loved, I had to walk away from something without being fully aware of whether or not it would even be worth it. As in previous times when the opportunities to obey God presented themselves, confirmation that I made the right choice to obey was waiting for me right around the corner...*after* I relocated.

In the fall, ministry school began. As students, we were immediately challenged to step out of our comfort zones and begin to pray for those who needed healing. We especially needed the practice because in a few weeks we would join Randy Clark, a healing evangelist who was the apostolic leader of our school, in Brazil for ten days to be part of his ministry team.

That made me nervous. I still was scared out of my mind to pray for people who needed physical healing. However, all it took was a little homework assignment to shock me into the reality that I was past the point of no return. We were all asked to find someone who needed prayer for healing and pray for them. That's all. We didn't actually have to see them healed. We just had to pray for them.

One would have thought I was being asked to swallow a sword in front of a thousand-person audience. I literally panicked, but as I got in my car, I was reminded that if God was the One who told me to attend this school, He planned to be the One to help me as I fulfilled the requirements for this assignment.

I asked God where to go, and He put a place on my mind. I "saw" nothing more than the location, so I fastened my seatbelt and drove to this local store just a few miles from the school. Now, I have always tried to follow the rules, and it made me nervous to just go praying for people in this store without some form of managerial permission. This sounded like a word of wisdom from God, so I approached a manager and explained to her that I attended an area ministry school, and I was practicing praying for people's healing. I asked her if I could pray for any of her employees who needed healing.

I braced myself for the big "Are you crazy? Absolutely NOT!", but to my surprise I got "Sure. Just don't make anyone receive prayer unless they want it." That sounded like a plan to me. I started roaming the store trying not to draw suspicion. I felt awkward and my heart was literally about to burst out of my chest. It took everything within me not to run out to the parking lot, jump in my car, and drive away at Mach speed. Then, I saw an employee stocking shelves, and I decided she was going to be the one that would help me break this cycle of my trepidation of praying for healing.

I approached her and told her the same thing I discussed with the manager a few moments earlier. Once again, I was expecting a flat out, "No!" However, she replied, "I was getting ready to go to the break room to take pain medication for my knee right now. I have had chronic knee pain for a while, and it's really bad today. I would love for you to pray for me, but I am on the clock, and I don't think I can let you." Thankfully, I listened to God's wise counsel earlier when I walked into the store, and I knew her manager permitted me to pray for any of the employees whether they were on the clock or not. After explaining to her that I already had her manager's permission, she allowed me to pray for her. I prayed a short prayer, and nervously looked up to ask her the question I dreaded the answer to---*Have you noticed a change in your knee since I prayed?*

The ten seconds it took her to answer the question seemed more like ten years. She said, "It's fifty percent better. " "Wow!" I said, "Really?" My rookie, praying-for -healing -self was just as surprised as she was. I felt this faith build up in my system, and I asked her if I could pray for her again and see if God would heal the other fifty percent. I shocked myself. Who was this new Tara that was coming forth?

After praying for her a second time, she told me the pain had completely left and that she was no longer going to need to take her pain medication. I was so excited about what just happened that I don't even remember walking out of the store and back to my car. I sat in awe of God for a while in the parking lot and pondered how I had allowed fear to keep me from realizing the access I have to God's healing power, and that healing power operating through me to others.

As I continued to process what just happened, courage and faith filled me up where all the fear previously existed, and I mustered up the urge to call a friend who had been suffering with kidney issues. I prayed for her over the phone, and a heat started to manifest on her back in the area around her kidney, and the pain significantly decreased.

Now I knew that even if nothing more were to happen during this year of ministry school, God had transitioned me from the role of teacher in Virginia to the role of student in Pennsylvania in order to answer the desire He whispered to my heart a few months before. I knew that listening to that whisper had resulted in a breakthrough that would forever change both me as an individual and my ministry.

Also, after the healings during that one-hour ministry school assignment, I began to realize that even though obedience to God's call for me to attend ministry school required more from me, it was also requiring more from God. He was delivering on His word to me. When He asked me to take a gamble with my comfortable life as a Virginia teacher, He planned to put all His chips in too. Like the little boy who helped Jesus feed thousands[10] in one day, I was only required to give Him my "loaves and fish." He fully planned to multiply them, and I was about to see that manifest full force as I, a rookie, healing –prayer-team member, embarked on the student mission trip to Brazil.

---

10 John 6:9-11

Chapter Six

Brazil

Near the end of one Randy Clark's healing services in Brazil, I, along with other ministry school students, served on the team who prayed for the sick. Shortly before we were called up to pray for those who would line up for ministry, I reflected on how God healed the woman with knee pain in that store in Pennsylvania just a few weeks before. Then, He whispered this thought to me:

> *Tara, this moment in Brazil is no different than that moment. No matter how difficult someone's need for healing may seem to you, pray for him or her the same way you prayed for the woman at the store.*

After that quick locker-room pep talk, the time to pray had come. I walked to the front of the church and turned to face the audience. With the other students who eagerly waited to pray for people, I watched as those needing healing lined up in front of each of us. Approximately forty people stood in front of me, but one man in particular caught my attention. Using crutches equipped with arm braces, he dragged himself to stand in line. I wondered if this type of physical malady was what God had been referring to earlier when He whispered *"no matter how difficult someone's need for healing may seem to you, pray for them the same way you prayed for the woman at the store"* but I set that aside for the moment and focused on the person in front of me.

The person currently standing in front of me was a woman who had an ailment that, in my opinion, was an "easy" one for God to heal. She had a knee problem, and because of my recent experience while doing my homework for the ministry school, I knew beyond a shadow of a doubt that God heals knees! I was thankful that this was the first person in my line requesting prayer, and that the man with the crutches was fifth in line. I figured this would give God a little time to warm up His healing skills before I got to the more difficult case.

With complete faith, I prayed for the woman with the knee problem, and God took all of her pain away. On down the line I went. With each person I prayed for, God healed them including a woman who had a tumor, which completely dissolved beneath my hand as I prayed. Although my faith was building with each person healed, I was fully aware that I would soon be standing in front of that person---the man that seemed "too difficult" for God to heal, the man with the crutches. Before I knew it, he stood in front of me.

He explained that he needed prayer for two things—pain in his back and partial paralysis in his legs. He told me that he had been shot in the back multiple times, and that the bullets could not be removed because that could lead to complete paralysis of the legs. As a result, he lived in constant back pain. The bullets and the swelling they caused left him unable to walk without the aid of crutches. He literally used the crutches to drag himself wherever he went.

I told him that I would pray for his back first. He didn't know this, but I was trying to keep up my momentum of faith for his healing, and once again, I started with what I assumed would be easier for God. I prayed for his back, and the pain instantly left. With that healing, he thanked me and began to drag himself back to his seat. I put my hand on his shoulder and said, "Wait. You wanted me to pray for God to heal your legs and the paralysis too."

Looking at the floor in shame, he said, "I don't have enough faith for God to heal my legs. I will wait until I do to receive prayer." Right then, I felt this faith well up in me, and I remembered God's whisper to me before the prayer ministry began. I asked the man receiving prayer if he would just lean on my faith for the moment, and if he would be willing to just give prayer a try. With a shrug of his shoulders and a half-hearted "Yes", he gave me permission to pray for him again.

I have no idea what came over me at this point, but I literally felt this extra measure of faith well up within me. I prayed for him for only about twenty seconds, and then I asked him to test out his legs. He said, "But I can't walk. How can I test them out?" I said, "I just prayed for your healing, so I believe you can walk. Just test it out." He took one step forward and then another. Then, his whole countenance changed and he began to walk full strides while holding his crutches. Then, as he realized he was completely healed, he handed me his crutches and began to run around the room as people cheered and praised God for his healing!

As if this was not amazing enough, God healed every person in my prayer line that night. He healed knee pain, removed a breast tumor, wiped out paralysis and so much more. What an unforgettable night of miracles!

One thing God has consistently impressed upon me since that night is that those miracles did not actually begin that night. They began a year earlier when I had decided to apply for ministry school after reading Mark 16 and wondering why I wasn't seeing miracles manifest through me. That moment one year earlier was my "burning bush" where God asked me to turn aside and hear His instruction. The seeds of desire He placed on my heart at that time combined with my obedience to leave my job and go to school, led to this moment in Brazil where God did amazing things in and through me---He healed forty people! Don't forget---All of this happened a mere six weeks after I overcame my fear to pray for God to heal!

I used to worry about what would happen if I prayed for people and no change occurred in their bodies. After Brazil, I am more concerned that an amazing demonstration of God's love will not be experienced if I am too afraid to step out and obey. I refuse to live in fear of failure anymore. Instead, I would rather choose to live in a place of anticipation of the goodness of God being made manifest in others' lives through me and other people who believe in Him. That kind of mentality is so much more freeing than fearing failure. I figure the only thing that held me back from seeing God's miracles the first three decades of my life was a big two-letter word---ME.

Returning to Pennsylvania from Brazil, I was super-charged and ready to pray for anyone who needed healing, but my faith and obedience were about to be tested. Once a dear friend told me, "Your faith isn't true faith until it is tested" and I was about to find out what that really meant. What I knew to be true in Mark 16 was now in the boxing ring with my circumstances and it appeared my circumstances were winning the match.

Chapter Seven

The Test of Contradiction

God allowed me a couple of months to nurture the seeds of the whisper He planted in my heart while I was still a high school teacher in Virginia. Those whispered seeds challenging me to connect my belief in Jesus for His miracles were now emerging through the soil of my heart. God graciously guarded them from anything that could scorch them before they were strong enough to take complete root. I finally possessed faith that miracles could be released through the average Joes or Josephines like me, and I naively figured nothing could knock me off my faith cloud at this point. But, the honeymoon period of my faith was about to collide with contradiction.

In December 2010, three months after that miracle filled trip to Brazil, I sat with my friend Tamela at lunch one Sunday. She shared with me that she had found an abnormal growth on her body and would be going to the doctor to get it examined. We prayed together, and agreed that it was probably nothing to worry about. Little did I know, but that lunch would be the last time I would spend with my friend before the dark cloud of cancer loomed over her. A few days after our lunch, Tamela's husband Neil called me to tell me that Tamela had just been diagnosed with stage four uterine cancer, and without a miracle from God, she only had 6-8 months to live.

Immediately, I drove the two hours to be with my friend in her darkest hour. This faith, obedience, and response to God's whispers, especially in the area of healing, had just become personal---very personal. It became personal when all the prayer chains, friends, and family members were contending for healing. It became personal as she progressed through radiation and chemo. It became personal and as I watched her continue to trust God for her life as her body began to waste away as she fought hard and strong. It became most personal when she died just as the doctors predicted. Then all the questions ensued. Why doesn't everyone get healed? Why did the woman with the knee pain in Brazil get healed but my precious friend with two little girls and a husband lose their mom and wife? Why did God heal strangers in Brazil, but not my friend?

A few months before Tamela passed away, I shared a meal with her to celebrate her upcoming birthday. This actually happened on the day I would be boarding a plane for a mission trip to Thailand. After laughing and reminiscing with her for those few precious hours, I hugged her and said my good-byes. I was all too aware that this might be the last time I would ever see her alive.

The realization that I may have just spoken with one of my best friends for the last time weighed upon me as I made my way through check-in and airport security. After I boarded my flight, I was finally able to allow the tears to freely flow. I couldn't believe that I was leaving to minister in a country where I would most likely be asked to pray for people's healing. This was especially difficult knowing that in the hours before I left for Thailand, one of my last conversations with my friend included a weighty moment where I said everything I would want to say in the event my friend passed away before I came home. That was my send off to Thailand.

My faith in God as Healer was radically tested as I wrestled with the reality of my last moments with my friend whose now emaciated body had been ravaged by cancer, radiation, and chemo, and whose thick auburn hair--her crown of glory--had been replaced by shiny bald scalp and fisherman's cap. Those images haunted me as I traveled to Thailand and as I walked the streets of the red light district there. In Chiang Mai, I wanted to see miracles. I asked God to help me still believe for them even though I had the painful contradiction of my dying friend at the forefront of my heart the entire trip. He was faithful to answer that prayer.

One evening I, along with my ministry team, walked into a bar where prostitutes were beginning to welcome their customers for the evening. I noticed one woman in particular sitting at the bar. Her arm was wrapped in an Ace bandage, and she looked like a prime target for healing prayer. Along with my friend and fellow missionary, Kay, we approached the woman. I asked her why she was wearing a bandage on her arm, and she explained to us that she had been riding her motorbike the previous evening and had fallen off of it, either severely spraining or breaking her arm. She had no money to go to a doctor, but could not move her wrist without pain or make a fist with her hand.

I asked her if she knew who Jesus is. She said she did not, so I asked her if I could tell her about Him. She allowed me to share the gospel with her. Then, I asked her, "Now that you know who Jesus is, would you like to experience Him?" I asked her if she would be willing to take off her bandage and allow me to pray to Jesus to heal her. She promptly took off the bandage and held out her bruised arm. Kay and I gently took her hand and prayed a short twenty-second prayer. She stepped back from us after the prayer and she said that when we prayed, she felt heat go through her arm and her pain disappeared. I asked her to move her arm and to make a fist, and she was able to do both. All the while others in the bar looked on in amazement as her cast was lying on the bar behind her.

This healing seemed so effortless. It was as effortless as the ones in Brazil or the ones at the store in Pennsylvania. Of course I struggled with the *whys* as I dealt with the reality of God's healing happening everywhere but the place I would have given my right arm to see it--my friend Tamela's bedroom. I didn't understand why God would heal a prostitute in Thailand but not a mother of two little girls and one of my best friends. However, I also knew that I wouldn't trade the woman's healing in the bar for Tamela's healing. I wanted God to heal them both, but that wasn't happening. This was a mystery to me, and I figured I would always have these types of mysteries in my life. However, I knew if I wanted to see God continue to heal people on this trip in Thailand, I would have to continue to ask for His grace to obey His voice as I wrestled with these mysteries. I wanted to still yield myself to God and His whisper a year before that went something like this:

> *Go to ministry school and learn to walk out Mark 16--*
> *I want My people to believe in me and lay hands on*
> *the sick and see them healed.*

In this moment, I had two choices. I had to choose whether my experiences would dictate my theology, belief and obedience to that whisper He had spoken to me or if God's Word would continue to drive my actions throughout life. I could have easily withheld my prayers for anyone else and given up praying for healing as an act of anger against a God who seemingly planned to "take" my friend, or I could believe that the only thief is Satan. I chose to believe what Jesus revealed in John 10:10 when He said, "The thief comes only to steal and kill and destroy. I [Jesus] came that they may have life and have it abundantly." Also, I opted to believe James 1:17 that describes God as the "Father of Lights" and a "Giver of every good and perfect gift," not a taker of them.

After returning home from a this trip to Thailand where God continued to heal emotionally and physically, I resolved that neither God nor Tamela would want me to stop praying for others who needed healing. Just a few months after returning home, my decision to not allow my circumstances to dictate my theology on God's love and power, was immediately tested again after Neil called to tell me that Tamela had passed away.

I hung up the phone after that difficult call, and before I started the grieving process, I wanted the first prayer out of my mouth to be "Father, by Your grace, I will not allow this to stop me from praying for those who need healing, and especially for those who need healing from cancer." This was not an easy prayer, but I knew if I didn't at least say it, I would be tempted in the future to never walk out that declaration. So, amid the grief and pain of the loss of my precious friend, I committed to believe in a God who whispered to me a year before that He wanted me to pray for the sick.

Can you imagine what Satan does when his robbery and destruction do not unravel a heart committed to obeying God regardless of the cost, the contradiction faced, or the obstacles? He flees in the midst of that kind of resistance, but that kind of resistance is not possible without strengthening ourselves in the Lord and leaning upon His grace.

In this resistance during contradiction, I realized in an even greater way, that if I was really serious about responding to God's whispers, it was going to require a commitment on my part even when outcomes did not make sense, appeared impossible, or seemed to be the opposite of what I would desire. This is when the proverbial rubber met the road, and for a good long while, every time I prayed for someone's healing, thoughts of Tamela were not far behind. As I would pray for people to be healed, God never failed to comfort me within the contradiction and the mystery.

During this season, I began to consider so many people in the Bible who experienced contradiction in the midst of obeying what they thought God had said. Once God shut the door to the ark that Noah built, it didn't rain for seven days.[11] Because of the evil in that day,[12] Noah quite possible had to listen to the ridicule of those outside the ark and deal with their insults for an entire week as he waited for God to come through and stay true to His word. What

---

11 Genesis 7:10

12 Genesis 6:5-6

must he have been thinking? Did it ever cross his mind in those seven days, "Did I miss God?"

In the same way Noah found himself in the midst of contradiction, Joseph was tested as well. Immediately after receiving words from God about his destiny, he was sold into slavery and then sent to prison.[13] Next, I considered David. He was anointed to be king of Israel and then immediately sent to go back to take care of a bunch of smelly sheep.[14] Then, he was hunted by the king and viewed as a traitor.[15] What about Abraham? He raised his promised son into adolescence before God asked him to sacrifice him on Mount Moriah. I thought of Job, a faithful servant of God, who was tested, who lost so much, yet God restored all he lost and more.[16] In all of these examples, the seeds of their faith and obedience were quickly followed by contradiction. Without their steadfast obedience, they would have failed to see the fulfillment of what God had initiated in them.

In seasons of contradiction, we build the muscles to shoulder the fulfillment of all that God has begun in us. Our radical obedience, even when we don't understand, is what opens us up to the reality

---

13 Genesis 37, 39-47

14 1 Samuel 16:1-13

15 1 Samuel 23

16 Job 1:8-12, Job 42:10

that Jesus is not only the Author of our Faith but also the Finisher of it. Had Noah given up on the sixth day of no rain, he and his family would have perished along with the rest of the world. If Joseph had given up in the prison, his family and the entire land would not have been preserved in the midst of famine. Had David given in to pride and resisted going back to feed sheep after being anointed King, Israel would have continued to suffer under the leadership of Saul, and David would have forfeited the blessing of being in the ancestry of Christ.[17] If Abraham had disobeyed in the midst of contradiction, he wouldn't have seen the fulfillment of God's promise that he would be the father of many nations.[18] If Job had cursed God as his wife suggested[19], he would have forfeited the opportunity to demonstrate his love and commitment to God and missed the blessing of seeing an epic restoration that exceeded all that he had lost.

I learned in the loss of Tamela and through these Biblical examples, that the roots of the seeds that God plants in our hearts through His whispers are most often cultivated and pruned in lonely fields filled with sheep, dark prison cells, or surrounded by naysayers. Contradiction seems to be a part the lives of people who obeyed God at an exponential cost. However, just like the

---

17 Isaiah 11:1

18 Genesis 17:1-6

19 Job 2:9

father's of our faith, if we hold fast to God's words by not only hearing but obeying even in the contradiction, our reward will exceed anything lost in our the time of testing.

Chapter Eight

Aftermath of Contradiction

The death of my dear friend was like the moment that the Egyptian magician's rods turned into snakes just like Moses'.[20] I wonder what it must have been like for him, standing in front of all those people in Pharaoh's throne-room and wondering if God had stood him up when it mattered most. When everyone was watching and ready to disprove Moses' God, it appeared that the God of Moses had failed and contradicted His own words. However, it wasn't long before God showed up in a mighty way and proved that He was stronger than any magic when He caused Moses' rod to eat all the snakes of the magicians.

On that summer trip to Thailand, I witnessed miracle after miracle, but three months after returning home, I attended Tamela's funeral. In the midst of all of the contradiction I was not without opportunities to still trust that God is Healer despite what my circumstances seemed to say. About three months after the

---

20 Exodus 7:12

funeral, on Christmas Day in Southeast Asia, I ministered at a house church there via Skype for their Sunday morning service. God's whisper came before I made the call. He ever so quietly spoke:

> *I am Emmanuel. God with them. And I am going to them that I am with them by healing them.*

It was at this time that I had a choice. Do I still yield to the whisper? Do I still obey when watching my friend slowly die and seeing her little girls follow her casket out of the church had tainted my childlike faith. Do I still trust even within this mystery of God planning to heal people over the Internet after not healing my friend?

By God's grace and grace alone, I decided to trust. At this point in my life, I felt like I had gone too far to turn back now. I had seen God be faithful to heal so many times that I knew He did heal, and I refused to allow Tamela's death to shout louder than His whisper.

Once the Skype call connected, I gazed at a video screen capturing the spiritually hungry room where everyone in attendance could be persecuted by government officials for having such a meeting. Many in the room were Buddhist, and that didn't bother God at all. He is Emmanuel for them, too. Jesus was born to reconcile them to the Father and to be their Healer, and He was about to show that to them in a mighty way.

I preached about who God is as Emmanuel (just as He had whispered to me), and I said He was going to heal people to show that He is their Emmanuel. Minutes later, something went wrong with the Internet connection, and the call disconnected. I had to wait several days to find out if people were actually healed as God promised. Then, the reports started to come in. In total, there were fourteen people healed after the call failed. One of the persons healed was a Buddhist man and he waited three days to report his healing because he could not believe it had happened. He had a chronic ear issue that God completely healed.

One thing I learned in all of this is that Jesus heals prostitutes, Buddhist men, and, on the other side of heaven, my dear friend Tamela. Not even the loss of Tamela changed the fact that He was and is Healer. That's why I have chosen to obey in the mystery of the *whys,* and I know that when I do, Emmanuel will show Himself faithful every time.

Since Tamela passed away in 2011, over seventy people have been physically healed as God has flowed with His healing power as I have prayed for them. It pains me to even think about the fact that those seventy would not have experienced God as Healer if I had withheld my obedience and childlike trust in the midst of contradiction. Wrestling with mystery is sometimes a cost to obeying the whispers of God, but in the end, as we yield to His voice in the midst of those mysteries, God proves that He is more than worth the price we paid to follow Him.

Chapter Nine

Making Mistakes

Contradiction is not the only buzz kill we may face as we navigate the roads of obeying God's whispers. At some point in my journey, I realized that my obedience and faith had to become stronger than my fear of failure if I was ever going to see what He whispered materialize. I also had to face the reality that I may not always get it right, and I would have to back pedal, re-do, and sometimes even apologize.

Let's consider the disciples James and John. They were rightly labeled the "Sons of Thunder,"[21] and are described in Luke 9:51-56 in this incident that occurred on one of their "ministry trips" with Jesus:

> When the days drew near for him to be taken up, he set his face to go to Jerusalem. And he sent messengers ahead of him, who went and entered a village of the Samaritans, to make preparations for

---

21 Mark 3:17

him. But the people did not receive him, because his face was set toward Jerusalem. And when his disciples James and John saw it, they said, "Lord, do you want us to call fire down from heaven to consume them?" But he turned and rebuked them. And they went on to another village.

Here, Jesus and his "ministry team" were traveling to a town to minister to people, and the town rejected them. Upset by this, James and John devised a plan on how best to handle the situation---kill people. They assumed that God would want them to handle this situation the same way Elijah would have---by calling down[22] fire. What was Jesus' response? He gave them a very brief teaching explaining that the spirit in which they were operating was not appropriate. Then, He led them to another village and let them continue to minister. What? The greatest teacher of all time and our Savior allowed them to minister after such an act of blatant lack of compassion and love.

Later on in the disciples' journey with Jesus, Peter did something that was, in some people's opinions, much worse than what James and John did in this moment. He denied Christ three times.[23] After committing the sin we may label as one of the worst one could ever commit, Jesus invited Him to lead His followers ("Feed My

22 2 Kings 1:10

23 Luke 22:54-62

sheep").[24] Fifty days after he committed this horrible sin, he led the service at Pentecost and 3,000 people came into relationship with Jesus that day. [25]

In our modern churches, how would we have reacted to the Sons of Thunder or Peter? My guess is that in many churches, we probably wouldn't even allow them to collect the offering, much less minister. Is this what causes so many of us to be afraid to make a mistake when it comes to responding to God's voice? What if God is more concerned with the motives for our actions than the actual outcome? What if God is really more moved by us obeying what we think He *may* be saying, than by us not taking action because of fear of failure?

A friend of mine calls this fear the "paralysis of analysis." In a similar vein, I have heard a famous minister, Heidi Baker, say that our "heads are too big and our hearts are too small." In other words, oftentimes we allow logic, reason, and fear to talk us out of what God is directing us to do. Prior to my learning to respond to God's whispers, I wasted so much time being afraid of failure that I had paralyzed myself from acting on many thoughts that were most likely God speaking to me. As a result, I lived in a reality

---

24 John 21:15-17—Jesus invites Peter to feed His sheep (followers) three times. (The same amount of times He denied Christ)

25 Acts 2:41

where my head remained big with all kinds of ideas, but my heart remained atrophied from not following it.

My smashingly successful date with Jesus in 2001 began my journey of listening to His whispers and actually acting on them. However, I also had to face times when I either failed or things did not work out exactly as I had anticipated. Yet, I still live to tell about it. One of these happened on my way back from a ministry trip in Brazil.

I was waiting at my gate to take a red-eye flight back home from an amazing second ministry trip to Brazil in 2010. As on the first trip when God healed the paralyzed man, God moved in great power as well on this trip. Needless to say, I was boarding the plane with an ever-deepening faith in God's willingness to perform miracles.

Because I was getting ready to board the redeye flight back to the U.S., a simple request slipped from my mouth as I waited at the gate. I prayed, "It sure would be nice to have a row of seats to myself so I can just stretch out and sleep." Shortly after that, I boarded my flight, and quickly realized my prayer that had not been answered.

I climbed over a young man in my row to get to my seat. He was wearing headphones, and I was thrilled that if I had to sit next to someone on a red-eye, he would at least be listening to his music and not wanting to chat with me. As soon as I thought that, he removed his headphones and started talking. As people continued to board, he shared with me how he had a terrible ringing in his ears and that this had been a chronic issue since he was five years old.

Upon hearing this information, I heard what I *thought* was a God whisper. I had this idea pop in my head to say, "When that ringing in your ears goes away by the end of this flight, will you allow me to tell you why?". Chalk it up to being extremely zealous after seeing God heal so many people in Brazil, but my presumptuous self blurted that out to the man next to me.

His response was not what I expected. He said, "Why? Are you a voodoo priestess or something? Are you going to heal me?" I laughed and asked him if he thought I looked like a voodoo priestess. I don't think either one of us knew what a voodoo priestess looked like, but somehow he didn't know how else he could be healed on that plane. After an awkward conversation, he agreed to let me know if he was healed and I agreed to tell him why that happened when it did.

Right then, the captain came on the loud speaker and announced that we were going to be stuck at the gate for a while because there was a mechanical issue with the plane. A couple of hours later, we were still at the gate, and the man next to me had fallen asleep. When he woke up, I asked him if the ringing in his ears had left yet.

He was agitated and in a snippy tone told me the ringing in his ears had not gone away. As he groggily looked around the plane and realized we were still at the gate, he promptly unbuckled his seat belt, stood up, and ripped his luggage from the overhead bin while all the while loudly demanding to be let off the plane. A flight attendant tried to calm him down, and he pointed at me and told her that he was sitting next to a crazy woman and that he did not want to be next to me or on the plane anymore. After several minutes of commotion between him and the flight attendant, he was removed from the plane by the Brazilian version of the TSA.

Meanwhile, on the other side of the plane, a friend of mine was praying for other passengers during our long delay and at least one person had been healed. I, on the other hand, was causing the plane to be delayed further, as they sent a TSA officer on the plane to pull the cushions from my row to make sure the man who had just made a grand exit had not left a bomb behind. After a search of my row and a confirmation that the mechanical issue had been fixed on the plane, the main cabin doors were shut and we taxied down the runway.

I felt the shame of disappointment and failure wash over me. My faith-filled bubble was busted, and so was I! I knew I had missed it. I had misheard or misinterpreted God's whisper. I promptly repented with a sheepish "God I am so sorry. I was just so excited and figured you were going to heal that man. I am so sorry that I jumped too quickly and assumed. Please forgive me."

I was expecting God to give me a convicting tongue lashing at that point. I figured He was going to shout this time instead of whisper. I prepared for the worst, but He jokingly said, "Well, You did ask for a row all to yourself."

What?!? I had failed. I had been presumptuous. I had acted on what I thought was His voice but may not have really been. And, initially, all He had was a joke for me? I knew that He knew that I had misinterpreted His voice, but that seemed immaterial to Him at that moment. Instead, I felt His joy and pleasure that I had obeyed what I thought He was saying. He was more concerned with my motive than He was with the outcome. He knew my heart was to bring Him glory even if that put me in the awkward situation of waiting for a man to be healed for hours on a flight from Brazil to the U.S.

This is by no means a story to give us the excuse to act frivolously or presumptuously when it comes to God's whispers, but it revealed to me that He is more concerned with our hearts and motivations than anything else. If I had said those things to my fellow passenger out of my own pride or selfish desire to look cool or like some mega-healer-evangelist, I am sure that God's response would not have been a joke, but a rebuke the likes of which James and John received when they wanted to call down fire on people.

However, even with that rebuke, if I followed it with my repentance, His grace would come. Just like a loving father with his child, I am sure I would have been allowed to get back on my bike and try riding again. But I would just have my training wheels and helmet the next time. And, true to God's character, there was a next time for me at a bar in the red light district of Thailand.

Chapter Ten

My "Next Time"

Just like James, John, and Peter, I was given many more "next times." Next times to hear God's whispers and obey. Next times to try and fail. Next times to experience outcomes the opposite of what I would have expected or witness more than I dreamed.

God doesn't ask us to be perfect. He just asks us to be the best possible stewards of the seeds that He gives us. In 2 Corinthians 9:10, we are admonished that "He [Jesus] who supplies seed to the sower and bread for food will supply and multiply your seed for sowing and increase the harvest of your righteousness." To whom does Jesus provide seed? The sower—the person who invests in what He gives him or her. The bottom line is that obedience, no matter the outcome, leads to more adventures in God.

Lets consider the parable of the seed in Mark 4:26-29:

> And He [Jesus] said, "The kingdom of God is as if a man should scatter seed on the ground. He sleeps and rises night and day, and the seed sprouts and

grows; he knows not how. The earth produces by itself, first the blade, then the ear, then the full grain in the ear. But when the grain is ripe, at once he puts in the sickle, because the harvest has come."

In this story, Jesus teaches a concept related to sowing the seed that He gives us. He explains that obedience to releasing His kingdom is like a *man* planting seed. Notice, He doesn't say a *farmer* (who would be an expert at planting seed). When He uses *man* instead of *farmer*, could He be suggesting that we don't have to be an expert to plant the seeds He gives us? Would He give seed to a novice? This may very well be the case. In this passage, the man has no idea how the seed multiplies or grows, but it does, and as a result, a great harvest is reaped. Also, notice that the man is not asked to strategically place each seed one at a time into the ground. He is to *scatter* it. He is asked to broadcast it all around and wait for God's wind to blow it where it should be placed. The act we are being asked to do here is simple. All we have to do is dip our hands in the seed bag, scoop up the seed, and throw it. Even a child could do this.

God's whispers are seeds He plants in our hearts and when we scatter them, they are bound to grow and spring forth into a harvest. Sometimes we may plant seeds expecting certain level of harvest, and it doesn't quite turn out the way we expect, but God is the Lord of the Harvest. As long as we plant the seed, He will produce the outcome that He desires as the author and finisher of our faith.[26] This would be an important concept to remember during another one of my ministry trips to Thailand.

Over the last several years, I have traveled to Thailand on multiple mission trips. I have witnessed many miracles and God's love demonstrated in profound ways in Southeast Asia. On one of these mission trips, I found myself on the sidewalk outside of a bar chatting with a transgendered male prostitute who I will call "Li." I didn't require a God whisper to tell me that Li needed healing. His swollen cheeks shouted loud and clear that He needed a dentist, a miracle or both. His swollen cheek was due to an impacted tooth causing him excruciating pain.

I just "knew" God wanted to heal his tooth. At least that's what I thought the prompting to pray for him meant. This was one of those moments when God's whispers were combined with my assumptions, but God's plan varied quite drastically from my own expectations, as I was about to find out.

As far as I knew, Li had never experienced God's healing power, but I asked him if I could pray for his tooth and told him I believed God intended to heal him. He allowed me to pray for him on the sidewalk in front of the bar while people walked by and stared at this unusual scene. I placed my hand on his cheek and prayed.

---

26 Hebrews 12:2

When I asked him to try to open his mouth, something that was very painful for him before prayer, he felt no different. He was still in excruciating pain. I couldn't believe it. I was almost certain that when God whispered to me and told me to pray for Li, God was planning on taking away all of Li's tooth pain. Now, I was thinking things like:

> *I can't believe God just had me give this man false hope!*

> *Maybe I missed it and God wasn't telling me to pray for him.*

> *Where did I go wrong? Why would God have me pray for this man and not heal His tooth?*

After these thoughts flowed through my mind, I sensed God whisper again. He gently spoke:

> *Remember what Randy Clark (the apostolic leader of the ministry school I attended) said? He taught the students that 'Not everybody gets healed but everybody gets loved.' Ask this man if he knows what My love looks and feels like.*

I seriously thought that God was not in touch with what this man really needed. I thought Li would prefer healing for his tooth rather than receiving a hug from Jesus right now, but I went along with the plan. I asked Li if he knew what God's love looked or felt like, and he told me that he didn't. Then, I heard one of the craziest whispers from God yet in my journey of learning obedience. The whisper came in the form of this thought:

> *Tell him to look in your eyes if he wants to know what My love looks and feels like right now.*

At this point, I really thought either God had fallen off His heavenly rocker or I had really misheard Him. I figured things couldn't get any more awkward than they already were, so I proceeded with obeying. I asked this transgendered man in Thailand to look into my eyes, and to my surprise, he immediately gazed intently in my eyes like he was searching for hidden treasure. As he searched my eyes for Jesus, he began to cry and tell me he saw "It." I said, "What do you see?" And he said, "The love of God." I then did what felt most natural in that moment, and I hugged him. He did not let go of me for five minutes.

I was starting to understand where things went wrong and where they went right in this experience. I realized that God, for whatever reason, was more interested in healing Li's heart than He was in healing Li's tooth in this moment. I also realized that Li didn't seem to care about his tooth when he was clinging to me like a child amidst the backdrop of busy street filled with tourists, prostitutes, and loud bar music. Where I went wrong was in assuming that God wanted to heal his tooth in order to get to his heart. Where I went right was in obeying what I thought were

God's whispers even when the outcome failed to be what I expected as the whispers got weirder and weirder. As a result, a broken man received a powerful revelation of God's love for him.

A week later, I visited Li again. He no longer had the tooth issue because a dentist fixed that problem, but he still had the love God from the hug he received. I asked him if I could give him another hug and this one lasted longer than the first. He was so touched by the moment that he wanted a photo of us, and after developing the photo at a shop nearby, I delivered it to him the day I left Thailand.

I thought that night was the end of the story, and that I would probably never see Li again. I had truly stumbled through this obedience, and realized that even though I had misinterpreted God's intent, God had still accomplished His purpose. Little did I know, God had already written another story for Li and me seven months in the future.

Seven months later, I arrived back in Thailand on another ministry trip. One of my first objectives was to find Li at the bar and see how he had fared since our God encounter. It's always amazing to me how much changes in my life in between these trips to Thailand, and how so much remains the same in the red light district. It's as if the rest of the world is moving at the speed of light and those in the bars in Thailand are living in slow motion.

I passed by bar after bar where women and men sell their bodies and souls for survival. Some were still wearing the same dresses and shoes I saw them in seven months earlier. I saw the same men and women prostitutes sitting on benches eating noodle soup and waiting for their next customers or "boyfriends" from the West to be their "knight in shining armor" for at least the night.

I arrived at the bar where Li worked, and the bartender said he was in the back getting ready for the night. Knowing Li would want to see me, the bartender led me back to him. When I saw him, I reached out to hug him, but he winced in pain, and asked me to follow him to a back room. There, he opened his dress and showed me a bandage wrapped around his chest. It was soaking in blood. In broken English, Li explained to me that he had just had surgery to give himself breasts, and it clearly had not worked.

He was pale and scared, and I couldn't believe that of all nights I could have stepped back into his life, that night was the one. I felt like a mom whose child was gravely ill, and I knew that if someone didn't help him, Li would most likely bleed to death that night. I pleaded with him to go to a hospital with me, but because he was so terrified that he would lose his job if anyone had witnessed what I saw, he thanked me, but told me that he planned to just go home and rest.

It horrified me to think that this man was preparing to leave on his motorbike to go back to his tiny little room somewhere in the red light district, go to sleep, and never wake up. I kept fruitlessly begging him to let me help him, but he said he would be okay, and he rode away in the rain on his motorbike.

My translator and I stood there in shock. We had no idea where he lived, but we knew that if we failed to find him, he would surely die. We found two other transgendered prostitutes to help us. They knew Li and where he lived. So, I, along with my Thai translator and two men dressed as women, ran down the rainy back streets of the red light district on a mission to find Li.

We knocked on his apartment door, and he lethargically opened it, shocked to find us. He invited us in, and, despite the fact that he was on death's door, he entered into typical Thai hospitality mode and began serving us water and juice. I quickly interrupted this custom and said "I am your mother and you are my child and we are going to the hospital now!" I seriously didn't know what had come over me, but I knew that God cared whether this man lived or died. Maybe no one else in the world would have batted an eyelash if a prostitute in Thailand died that night, but God loved this man, and He knew Li's value.

As we headed out the door, something caught my eye. Li had decorated one of his cabinets with row after row of photographs---pictures of family, the king of Thailand, and seductive pictures of himself. In the middle of all of these hung the picture we had taken together seven months earlier. I pointed it out, and he said, "That's a night I will never forget."

This present night was also a night that Li and I would never forget. All of us –Li, myself, my translator, and the two other men dressed as women—rushed to the hospital. I'm sure we were quite a sight in the emergency room as we sat together waiting for Li to be checked out and sewn up. After the doctor successfully tended to Li's open wound, he gave Li orders to go home and rest.

God saved Li's life that night, and I learned that God had a lot more in mind than a man's tooth when He whispered to me long ago to turn aside and notice this man to pray for him. God knew that Li would be so touched by the love of God that he would memorialize it with a picture in his house. God also knew that I would be in that bar again seven months later when Li needed a mom, and this time, it would save his life. God also knew that even though He was revealing that He chose Li to be His son, Li would still not choose Him yet.

God's whispers to me regarding Li were intended to be seeds that would be scattered all over Li's life. At the time, the seeds did not germinate into a salvation. As far as I know, Li still works in a bar in Thailand, but he has a picture on his cabinet and an indelible imprint of that same picture of God's love on his heart. I believe that the Lord of the Harvest who whispered to me about Li surely has the capability to multiply that seed that I scattered in Li's life. My only responsibility was to obey God regardless of the outcome.

I have had many opportunities to ponder this experience since it happened, and I have realized how limited our perspective can be compared to God's. I have thought of those in the Bible who each had one moment of obedience that changed history. Just like I may never know how my one night at the hospital with Li will impact his life down the road, many of our fathers and mothers in the faith were not immediately privy, if ever, to the impact of their acts of obedience.

Think about these fathers and mothers of faith and their obedience:

> *Rahab's act of obedience landed her a spot in the ancestry of Jesus.*[27]
>
> *Joseph's acts of obedience rescued his family and an entire nation from death by famine.*[28]
>
> *Esther's act of obedience delivered her and her people from genocide.*[29]
>
> *Moses' mother's obedience paved the way for Moses to become the deliver of Israel in Egypt*[30]

---

27 Joshua 2, Matthew 1:5-16

28 Genesis 37-47

29 Esther 4:14-16, Esther 7-10

30 Exodus 2:3, Hebrews 11:23, Exodus 14

Mary and Joseph's obedience protected Jesus so that He could fulfill why He came to earth---to be our Savior. [31]

Although some of these fathers and mothers had more than a whisper to push them in the right direction, they still had a choice whether to obey or not. They had the same choice we do every day. Just like them, whether our acts of obedience change the history of one life in a bar in Thailand or, as in the case of Esther, an entire nation, the greatest joy is that we get to partner with God through our obedience to see His kingdom released in our day and time.

---

31 Luke 1:28, Matthew 2:13

Chapter Eleven

My Greatest Test Yet

There are so many stories that I could continue to share, but it made sense to end with this one for now. All the other opportunities I have had to listen to God's voice and obey built the faith in me for the story I am about to share. I have flailed along the last thirteen years since that date with Jesus. I have questioned God, feared failure, and experienced loss. I feared that God would not take care of me at times along the way. I experienced those impatient moments where I said every minute, "God, are we there yet?" and I am still waiting for the fulfillment of so many whispers written in my journals.

However, through all the sowing, watering, and harvesting of the seeds God has planted in my life, I have learned much and have grown stronger in order to shoulder future fulfillment of God's promises and dreams. It's all part of His grand design, just as this story of God whispering to me in Austin, Texas.

In June 2013, I flew to Austin, TX and was asked by my friend Ramy Antoun to speak at a local Christian worship service called "Unplugged." This event was coordinated by a group of extremely creative and talented people who are part of a ministry called Rev 1211. (www.rev1211.org) I found myself singing the last song in the worship set before I would be invited up to speak, and I was nervous. I wasn't nervous about speaking. By now, I had ministered like this a gazillion times and as a high school teacher for almost a decade, I had long lost my fear of public speaking. Prior to the service, I sensed that I was supposed to share on the power of forgiveness. This would not be the easiest of topics, but certainly not the most difficult either. Even the greatest skeptic or non-believer would acknowledge that it is good to forgive, so this was the "safe" part of my message. What I was afraid of was the whisper I heard from God three minutes before I got up to speak--- *And I want to heal shoulders and knees tonight.*

At this point, a myriad of thoughts were running through my head:

> *I don't even know if these people believe in this stuff. At least in Brazil, I knew people wanted healing. After all, I was on the ministry team at a healing service. This isn't a healing service. It is a worship service.*

> *There are 250-300 people here. What if I'm wrong and God doesn't heal people? That is going to be much more costly than the guy on the plane who didn't get healed or the prostitute whose tooth pain didn't leave.*

> *What if I am right and God does want to heal people?*

Then, I heard my name called, and it was time for action. I figured that if I was going to take the plunge of obedience, it needed to be right away. Otherwise, I would either talk myself out of it or conveniently forget to be obedient. So, before starting my message on forgiveness, I greeted the crowd like this:

> *Hi, my name is Tara Browder, and I am so excited to be in Austin, TX. Before I share tonight, I just want to say that I am sensing God wants to heal shoulders and knees tonight, so as I am speaking, pay attention to any pain leaving your bodies and I will check in and see if God has healed anyone after I am done with my message. Okay?*

Whew! I had done it. I had obeyed, and I hoped no one would kill the messenger. I was glad the house lights were so dim that I couldn't see the people in the audience. They were eerily silent. If a cricket had been chirping, we all would have heard it. I ignored the uncomfortable thickness in the air, and proceeded with the "safe" part of the message. I was in perfect peace until I realized halfway through my message that the hardest part of my obedience was yet to come. I was headed like a speeding locomotive to the dreaded "did God heal anyone?" question that I would present to the audience after my message.

The time came for the question I feared. I asked the audience if anyone felt God touch them and heal them that night. Twenty seconds later, I saw a hand raised in the near pitch-black lighting of the room. That had been the longest twenty seconds of my life! Several people testified that night that they had been healed of shoulder and/or knee issues, and two reported they felt a heat or electricity go through their bodies and pain leave when I said, "God is going to heal knees and shoulders tonight." At the exact moment of my obedience, God delivered on the word He spoke to me, and additional testimonies of healing were received in the weeks following the meeting.

God never stops whispering to us, and as we steward those whispers, He rewards us by upping the ante and showing His glory in even greater ways. I am continually amazed at the fact that He could heal all on His own, but He chooses to partner with us to release His power and love on the earth—all through simple acts of obedience that start with dates and quick thoughts.

Since that date with Jesus long ago, God has given me countless opportunities to listen to His whispers, most of the time in the form of thoughts, and to respond to them. I desire that my experiences and testimonies be a catalyst for you to experience the same types of adventures with God. As you read part two of this book, my prayer is that God will continue to stir in you the desire to step out in faith to His whispers and that you will obtain practical wisdom as to how to put your faith into action.

Part Two:

How to Begin Your Journey

Chapter Twelve

What Has God Whispered to You?

God has whispered regularly to me since that date with Jesus in 2001. Sometimes I have obeyed whole-heartedly, and other times I have obeyed with skepticism, doubt, and fear. The measure of faith required on my part to obey the whispers has increased over time. However, none of the whispers made it more difficult for God to fulfill His purposes through me as I partnered with Him. Isaiah 55:11 makes promises regarding the words of God.

> So shall my word be that goes out from my mouth; it shall not return to me empty, but it shall accomplish that which I purpose, and shall succeed in the thing for which I sent it. The word of God does not return void, and God has proved that time and time again.

It has become much easier to obey His whispers as I have given up my fear of failure or of what people will think of me if I fail. This journey's testimonies have increased and multiplied as I have obeyed and stewarded the words God has given me. No woman or man of great faith was ever exempt from growing in favor with

God and man. Even Jesus had to do that.[32] They all had small beginnings that prepared them for greatness. They all had their own personal "dates" with God. Consider these examples:

> *Before he could ever be the prophet whose words would ever fall to the ground Samuel had to be mentored by Eli and respond to God's voice when his name was called.*[33]

> *Before she went before the king to save her people, Esther fasted and prepared herself for an entire year.*[34]

> *Before they and their descendants could possess the promise land, Joshua and Caleb learned during forty years in the wilderness how to operate in an opposite spirit of the Israelites who wanted to return to Egypt.*[35]

---

32 Luke 2:52

33 1 Samuel 3:4-10, 1 Samuel 3:19

34 Esther 2:12, Esther 4:16, Esther 7:1-6

35 Numbers 14:24, 30

Before he slayed Goliath or he led Israel as their king, David fed sheep and wrestled a bear and lion to protect them.[36]

Before he became second in command in Egypt, Joseph used his gifts and talents in Potiphar's household and in a prison cell. [37]

Before he led nearly 3,000 people to God at Pentecost and his shadow was anointed enough to release God's healing power, Peter learned to walk on water to Jesus.[38]

You may be wondering if everyone is called to live this kind of life. Does God ask everyone to live a lifestyle of childlike faith and obedience? The answer is an emphatic "YES!" To some, that may be the greatest invitation you have ever received, and you are excited about the adventure with God. To others, it is the scariest invitation you have ever received. For me, it was a mixture of both.

Jesus said in John 15:10, "If you keep commandments, you will abide in my love, just as I have kept my Father's commandments

---

36 1 Samuel 17:34-37

37 Genesis 37-41

38 Acts 2:14-41, Acts 5:15, Matthew 14:22-23

and abide in his love." One of the greatest ways we can abide in God's love and demonstrate love to Jesus is to obey His voice the way He did. He chose to do nothing unless He saw the Father doing it.

Has God whispered something to you as He did to Samuel in the house of Eli? Has He promised you something as He did David or Joseph and asked you to be faithful in the small beginnings? Has He, as in the case with Peter, asked you to step out of the boat? Has He asked you to prepare yourself like Esther? Have you obeyed? Do you know how to obey?

The final chapters of this book and the prayer that follows them are designed to help you on your own journey of listening to and responding to God's whispers. Before reading the next chapter, spend some time with God and ask Him to search your heart as you answer the following questions:

> *When was the first time you remember having faith and obedience like a child with God? What was the result? How has that affected your future steps of faith and obedience?*

> *Ask God to remind you of a time you obeyed His whisper and what the result was. Thank Him for that moment in time when He was true to His word as you partnered with Him.*

Ask God to remind you of His most recent whisper(s) to you and write them down.

Chapter Thirteen

Steps to Obeying His Whispers

Before writing this section of my book, I had a bit of hesitancy because I see God as creative who has personalized all of our unique journeys of obedience to His whispers. Some of us have needed a whale like Jonah[39] to assist us in obeying. Others have required the training ground of a field of sheep as in the case of David or a prison cell in Egypt as in the case of Joseph to teach us skills that will enable us to shoulder the fulfillment of God's promises. Thus, I tend to avoid giving anyone a formula for obeying God. The following is merely a pattern that I have observed in my own journey of obeying His whispers. These steps may be a helpful tool for you as you pursue Him in your own journey, but God may modify your journey to fit the unique desires He has for you.

---

39 Jonah 1:17

Steps to Hearing and Obeying God's Whispers

1. God Whispers

2. Record the Whispers

3. Seek Counsel

4. Prayer

5. Step Out

6. Follow the Favor

7. Thankfulness

Chapter Fourteen

Step One: God Whispers

The first step to responding to God's whispers is to position ourselves to hear them. Revelation from God is birthed out of intimacy and rest with Him. Therefore, if we want to hear His whispers, we have a posture to maintain before Him. That posture is defined by rest and daily time with God.

As a society, we, for the most part, have lost the art of truly resting. We can't just sit and daydream at an intersection while waiting for a red light anymore. From stoplight to stoplight, we send a quick text, respond to our email or check Facebook for the latest updates or Instagrams. Looking down at our phones has replaced looking up and chatting with someone in front of us in a line at the bank, and being anything other than instantly accessible to everyone is unacceptable. If people can't reach us by phone, shortly we will receive a text, and if we still are missing in action, we will get the email that starts with "Did you get my call or text?"

We have all given in to the monster of multi-tasking at one time or another, and we have given in to the pull to be online and available at all times. In fact, we are often rewarded for it. What boss doesn't want a great multi-tasker on his or her team? What person doesn't love to be able to say that they sent an email, ordered a birthday gift for a friend on Amazon, and drank their morning coffee all during their thirty-minute drive to work. Multi-tasking makes us feel accomplished, but as we dust off our hands and proudly move on to the next project, we fail to realize something. This multi-taksing is robbing us of true rest that our minds, bodies, and spirits need. It's also robbing us of time to hear God's whispers.

The truth is God never designed us to be full time multi-taskers. Of course there are going to be times when we need to do multiple things at once. Ask any mom who has held her child, stirred the spaghetti sauce on the stove, and answered the phone at the same time. However, we are not designed to be operating on eight cylinders 24 hours a day, seven days a week.

Think about this. Was God a multi-takser when He created the universe---a task that one could argue is one of the most difficult projects anyone could ever tackle? Even during the creation of the world, God, Himself, took time to take in each moment. He created one thing at a time and savored each and every thing He created by pausing, stepping back and savoring, and saying "It is good."[40] Perhaps we could learn from how He stopped and smelled the roses.

---

[40] Genesis 1

Speaking of creation, what was the first thing God did with Adam after He created him on the sixth day? He *rested* with him on the seventh day.[41] I believe this rest was to set the tone for man's relationship with God. How are we to live in between birth and our entry to heaven? We are to live in and from a place of rest with God---the place where His whispers are heard. As Christians, we struggle to not only rest in God but with God, and just as He did with Adam, He is calling us to rest with Him.

God has often reminded me that in addition to "Do not Murder", another one of the Ten Commandments is "Honor the Sabbath and Keep it Holy." [42] Therefore, rest and Sabbath are just as important to God as not murdering! As a result, being diligent to enter God's rest as described in Hebrews 4 must be one of our top priorities, just as it was with Adam and God in the Garden of Eden. Hebrews 4:9-11 says,

> So then, there remains a Sabbath rest for the people of God, for whoever has entered God's rest has also rested from his works as God did from his. Let us therefore strive to enter that rest.

If God, Himself, rested, it would be arrogant to think that we don't need to follow in His footsteps. Since creation, He has been beckoning us to rest in Him and with Him. After all, in order to

---

[41] Genesis 2:1
[42] Exodus 20:8, 13

hear a whisper, all other noises and distractions must come to a halt.

It is from this place, that God has designed our life to flow. So many worship with the idea that they are worshiping so that they can get into the presence of God. Because He never leaves us or forsakes us,[43] in actuality, we are really worshiping *from* His presence already. What would it be like to worship Him *from* His presence instead of using worship as the tool *to get into* His presence? This haven of rest is where He is always with us and we hear His voice and whispers most clearly. In reality, this place is a place we can live from instead of just a location we aim to get to for an hour a day. One way we can live from His presence is to slow down and eliminate as much multi-tasking, noise, and distractions as we can from our lives.

In addition to removing distractions and noise, what else positions us to hear someone whisper? We have to be close to the person releasing them. This is why it is so important to spend regular time in God's word and in conversation with God. In scripture, there are few actions we are admonished to perform daily, but one of them is praying for our "daily bread" as Jesus talks about in Matthew 6:11. This daily bread, however, is much more than something to fill our stomachs.

---

[43] Deuteronomy 31:6

The concept of retrieving our daily bread is observed as far back as when the Israelites were wandering the desert with Moses for forty years. In Exodus 16:4, the command God gave Moses and the people regarding daily bread is explained:

> Then the Lord said to Moses, 'Behold, I am about to rain bread from heaven for you, and the people shall go out and gather a day's portion every day, that I may test them, whether they will walk in my law or not.'

God provided manna (bread) and quail from heaven, but He required that the Israelites take action regarding that blessing. God could have dropped the manna directly in their tents, but He required them to get out of bed, walk out of their tents, and receive His blessing of fresh bread from heaven.

In the same way God required the Israelites to pursue the manna every morning, Jesus called us to pray for our "daily bread" in Matthew 6:11. Because of Jesus' coming to earth, "bread" became much more than something to satisfy our physical hunger, though. Through Jesus, who is called our "Bread of Life" in John 6:35, our daily "bread" is not just food; it is a person---the person of Jesus. So, when we are called to seek our bread daily, we are being called to seek The Bread---Jesus.

Jesus, our Bread, declared in Matthew 4:4 that "...man shall not live by bread alone, but by every word that comes from the mouth of

God." What if we really lived like our very life depended on hearing God's words? What if we valued His voice even more than the satisfying of our physical hunger?

One of my favorite books on this topic is *Can You Hear Me?: Tuning in to the God who Speaks* by Brad Jersak. He has a section in his book called "Answering Machine Prayers" and part of it reads as follows:

> For me, prayer amounted to leaving phone messages on God's answering machine. Faith was akin to hoping that God would eventually check his messages. The fruit of this attitude was terrible. It isolated me from personal friendship with God and instilled a hopeless fatalism into my prayer life."[44]

What if we saw prayer as not just sending God an email with our requests each day but more of a two-way communication between friends? God's whispers are birthed out of relationship, and the goal of spending daily time with God was never designed to be motivated from a need to solely "get things off of our chests" or desire to fulfill a religious duty. However, unfortunately, we can all get in a rut in our relationship with God and eventually our times with Him begin to look more like a venting session or religious

---

[44] Pg. 18 of 2003 Edition of *Can You Hear Me?: Tuning in to the God Who Speaks* by Brad Jersak.

duty than coffee between friends in mutual conversation. If it has become that way for you, I believe that will change as you approach each daily time with God as a new opportunity to not only speak to Him but to hear what He will whisper back you as well.

True intimacy is birthed out of a place of two people desiring to spend time together to get to know each other. If someone spends time with us just because they are required to, the depths of intimacy cannot be achieved. The soil of intimacy that whispers are birthed out of is fertilized with hunger, desire, and need.

If we define obedience as a religious act we do to earn God's love versus a way we worship and love God, our obedience to spend time with God getting our "daily bread" will be nothing more than religious slavery. That's why Jesus wanted to make it clear in John 15:14-15,

> You are my friends if you do what I command you. No longer do I call you servants, for a servant does not know what his master is doing; but I have called you friends, for all that I have heard from my Father I have made known to you.

In other words, our obedience should overflow from our friendship with God not out of an act of duty or obligation. We have access to His secrets if we position ourselves to hear them by being close to Him.

Chapter Fifteen

Step Two: Record the Whispers

Have you ever been to a restaurant and had a waiter or waitress who doesn't write down your order when they take it? More often than not, when this has happened to me, my order has not come to my table the way I asked for it to arrive. In fact, I even had this sense, as the waiter was taking the order that my burger was going to come with mustard on it even though I explicitly asked for no mustard---all because he or she didn't write it down.

On the flip side, when someone writes down what you say, it reveals they care about what you are saying. Shortly before my mom passed away, I had a phone conversation with her about just being hired for my first teaching job in Kansas City, MO. Shortly after I accepted the position, my mother passed away unexpectedly, and I made the trip back to Oklahoma City for her funeral. As I sat down on the couch to talk with my dad and plan the funeral, I noticed something. There was a pad of paper near the phone, and there were notes in my mom's handwriting on it. It read something like this:

Westport-Edison Senior Academy

Tigers

Blue and Yellow—School Colors

Teaching 9th and 10th Grade English

My heart started beating out of my chest and tears began to flow. Without my being aware, my mom had literally taken notes of one of our last conversations. She loved me and cared so much about the details of my life that she wrote them down, most likely, so she could tell others about her daughter and her daughter's new job. My heart swelled with this knowledge that my mom cared about my voice enough to write down what I said. Her written record spoke of how she valued me.

In the same way, God feels our love and value of Him when we record what He says, and as a result of our stewarding His voice, we end up hearing Him even more because He gives seed to the sower.[45] Jesus said "I do not live by bread alone, but by every word that proceeds from the mouth of God." Do we live like our life depends on the very words that proceed from God's mouth? Recording His words, whether it is in a journal or on a

---

45 2 Corinthians 9:10

Smartphone, is one of the first ways to acknowledge we care about and are stepping towards Him and His whispers.

Not only does writing down His words reveal our value of them, but it also ensures we won't forget them. Aren't you glad that the people of the Bible chose to right down their experiences with God and their words from Him? Their choice to write down and not forget God's faithfulness and His words ensured that not only they, but also generation after generation, would remember God. Also, keep in mind that had they not chosen to memorialize their experiences in writing, we would literally not have our holy scriptures and the life they bring!

Have you ever had a dream from God, woken up in the middle of the night and thought to yourself "I should write this down. Oh, I don't feel like getting up. I'll remember it"? Then, you wake up three hours later to your alarm and you remember you had a dream but very few, if any, of the details come to mind. No matter how God chooses to speak, it definitely behooves us to record it. For dreams, I record them on my phone and type them up later. For God thoughts during the day, I have a notepad I keep with me to write them down. Habakkuk was admonished to "Write the vision down and make it plain so that the people can read it and run with it."[46] In order to run with God's plans, we need to have

---

46 Habakkuk 2:12

them written down to refer to like a road map as we take steps toward Him and His will.

Chapter Sixteen

Step Three: Seek Counsel

Once the whispers of God reach our ears, when possible, and especially with big decisions like geographical moves, quitting jobs, taking jobs, buying a house, etc. it is important to seek counsel from close friends and pastors/leaders who walk in relationship with us. They help give advice on interpretation of God's words as well the application of the words. It is important that those we seek for counsel are ones who are willing to tell us the truth even if they feel it could cost relationship with us. We also must surround ourselves with friends who are not so impressed with us that they don't tell us the truth and they don't think the friendship can sustain them telling us the truth.

God uses people to sharpen us and filter words we believe are from God through scripture. Our friends and pastors have intimate knowledge of what are our blind spots and God uses them to protect us where and when we are shortsighted or blindsided. In the same way that hearing God's whispers cannot happen without regular communion with God, interpreting and applying His whispers cannot happen outside of community with other believers. In fact, God even whispers through the very ones who walk alongside us in the journeys throughout our lives.

Time and time again we see throughout scripture that God gave people ones who came alongside them to help in walking out God's instructions:

God is a triune God (God operates within "community")[47]

Adam and Eve[48]

Moses and Aaron[49]

David and Jonathan[50]

Esther and Mordecai[51]

Ruth and Naomi[52]

Jesus sending the seventy out in pairs[53]

---

[47] Genesis 1:26 ("Let us create man in our image...")

[48] Genesis 2:18-24

[49] Exodus 4:10-16, Exodus 17:12

[50] 1 Samuel 18:1-5

[51] Esther 4:14

[52] Ruth 1:16

[53] Luke 10:1

As in the case of all of these and many more in scripture, all of our journeys in obeying the voice of God are designed to be walked out within the framework of relationship with not only God, but with the Body of Christ----People. If we are not rightly aligned with the church and other Christians, we cannot be fully aligned with Christ. We cannot fully love God and hear Him clearly if we do not love and value His wife, and part of valuing the Bride[54] is valuing her counsel. At the end of the day, we are responsible to obey the voice of God regardless of any other voices; however, I will say that more times than not, those who God has sent to me to provide counsel and friendship throughout my life have helped me not jump the gun or give up when it appeared that I had missed it. They held my arms up when I was weary and were the "Moredecais" that gave me sound advice on how to walk out the words God had given me.

---

[54] Revelation 21:9

Chapter Seventeen

Step Four: Prayer

Listening to God's voice and responding to it should never be divorced from prayer. Two-way communication with God is key along the road to seeing God's words come to pass. Proverbs 16:3 says, "Commit your work to the Lord and your plans will be established." If we want our steps in His plan to be firmly established, we must first start out our journey by committing it to prayer.

One prayer that I pray as I begin to prepare to step towards a God whisper is I pray that the Spirit of God would guide and the spirits described in Isaiah 11:12-3 would surround me as I step out.

> There shall come forth a shoot from the stump of Jesse, and a branch from his roots shall bear fruit. And the Spirit of the LORD shall rest upon him, the Spirit of wisdom and understanding, the Spirit of counsel and might, the Spirit of knowledge and the fear of the LORD. And his delight shall be in the fear

of the LORD. He shall not judge by what his eyes see, or decide disputes by what his ears hear.

Isaiah, through these verses, prophesied what Jesus would be like. Jesus, being our model to follow, did not just walk in just the revelation of His Father, but in His wisdom, counsel, might, knowledge, and understanding as well. This gave Him the capacity to not judge by natural eyes or natural hearing, but rather, by His supernatural spiritual senses. This is the kind of wisdom, revelation and discernment we want from God as we inquire of Him on how to step toward His voice and obeying Him. When He answers the prayer for this kind of wisdom, He gives us divine strategy on how to obey His voice as well as wisdom on who to partner with to see it come to pass.

Chapter Eighteen

Step Five: Step Out

This is the step where the rubber meets the road. This is where we get to take the plunge and put our money where our mouth is so to speak. Jesus said, "Blessed, rather, are those who *hear* the word of God *and keep it.*"[55] Therefore, in God's eyes, there is no separation from hearing God's word and taking action on it.

The question is, what does the "stepping out" look like. Sometimes the steps will be baby steps like going on a date with Jesus and taking your credit card just in case He stands you up. Sometimes, it may be a bigger step like quitting your job and going to ministry school. However, remember, God didn't start me out by placing me in front of crowd of 200 or more people in Austin, Texas, asking me to release a word of knowledge for healing. He started me out at a country cookin' restaurant in Charlotte, NC on a date with

---

55 Luke 11:28

Him. He groomed me and prepared me for what He would be doing in my life years later. If I had not been able to trust Him for that date, I would never have been able to trust Him to take care of me financially when He asked me to leave my job. If I had not been able to trust Him when I prayed for the woman's knee in a store in Pennsylvania, I would have never been able to stand in front of a crowd in Austin, TX and declare that He was going to heal shoulders and knees.

It's in the baby steps we learn to trust Him more, and then we are willing to take the leaps when we know we have seen Him provide in the little jumps along the way. This is why every opportunity we get to step out in small or great ways is a joy. These steps allow us to steward what He whispers to us.

Sometimes all God is asking of us is baby steps at first. For example, from the time I was a teenager, I had received words about being called to international missions and ministry. However, it took time for the fulfillment of those words to come to pass. During the time between when His words are released to us and the fulfillment of those words, we are called to steward them and nurture them like seeds in a garden until the fruit comes and a harvest is produced.

Thus, even though I wasn't in a time of full release into missions, I knew God still wanted me to steward those words in the season I was in, so that's where the baby steps came into play. What were some of the baby steps that I took until fulfillment came? I got a passport. I learned a foreign language. I also helped with a house church for International students on my college campus. Through these little steps I stewarded the words God had given me about missions until He gave me the opportunity to make a big step towards missions when I went into full time ministry and planted a house church in Thailand in 2011.

As God whispers to us, one of the steps to responding to those whispers is to ask Him what steps we can take to respond to His voice immediately. Consider these two Bible stories that reveal this concept of taking steps of obedience:

The Feeding of the Five Thousand[56]:

> Now when Jesus heard this, he withdrew from there in a boat to a desolate place by himself. But when the crowds heard it, they followed him on foot from the towns. When he went ashore he saw a great crowd, and he had compassion on them and healed their sick. Now when it was evening, the disciples came to him and said, 'This is a desolate place, and the day is now over; send the crowds away to go into the villages and buy food for themselves.'
> But Jesus said, 'They need not go away; you give

---

56 Matthew 14:13-21

them something to eat.' They said to him, 'We have only five loaves here and two fish.' And he said, 'Bring them here to me.' Then he ordered the crowds to sit down on the grass, and taking the five loaves and the two fish, he looked up to heaven and said a blessing. Then he broke the loaves and gave them to the disciples, and the disciples gave them to the crowds. And they all ate and were satisfied. And they took up twelve baskets full of the broken pieces left over. And those who ate were about five thousand men, besides women and children.

All that was available to feed the people was five loaves of bread and two fish, but Jesus asked the disciples to feed the people. Their step was to get the fish and bread, bring it to Jesus, and let him bless it. That's all that was required of them. Jesus did the rest. As they obeyed Him and began passing it out, God multiplied what they had brought to Him. What we bring to the table will always be insufficient no matter how gifted we are. If we wait to be sufficient, it will never happen. Good thing scripture says, "Nothing is impossible with God."[57]

---

57 Luke 1:37

The Widow with the Oil[58]:

Now the wife of one of the sons of the prophets cried to Elisha, 'Your servant my husband is dead, and you know that your servant feared the Lord, but the creditor has come to take my two children to be his slaves.' And Elisha said to her, 'What shall I do for you? Tell me; what have you in the house?' And she said, 'Your servant has nothing in the house except a jar of oil.' Then he said, 'Go outside, borrow vessels from all your neighbors, empty vessels and not too few. Then go in and shut the door behind yourself and your sons and pour into all these vessels. And when one is full, set it aside.' So she went from him and shut the door behind herself and her sons. And as she poured they brought the vessels to her. When the vessels were full, she said to her son, 'Bring me another vessel.' And he said to her, 'There is not another.' Then the oil stopped flowing. She came and told the man of God, and he said, 'Go, sell the oil and pay your debts, and you and your sons can live on the rest.'

---

58 2 Kings 4:1-7

A woman's husband had just died, and the creditors were on the way to take her two sons to be slaves until the debt was paid. Elisha asked her what she had in her house that was available. All she had was one bottle of oil. He told her to go and get empty jars (he specified to get more than just a few) to be filled with oil to sell. That was all she was asked to do. She could have said, "No, there is no possible way this miracle could happen. You are crazy. I am not going to go get any jars. I am just going to go get a job." However, she obeyed the voice of God coming through Elisha, and God filled all of those jars with oil and provided for her with one simple act of obedience on her part---going door to door and asking her neighbors if she could borrow some empty jars.

No matter if the step is big or small, if God is the author of the whispers you are responding to, He promises to be the finisher of them.[59] Therefore, we can trust as we take steps of obedience we will see His favor and multiplication. Then, all we have to do is follow that favor.

---

59 Hebrews 12:2

Chapter Nineteen

Step Six: Follow the Favor of God

Once we begin to see God's favor, we need to respond to God's favor and multiplication with additional obedience. We must remember that God opens doors that no man can shut.[60] Even when we feel resistance in our journeys of obedience, we must trust that God opens doors that no man can shut and closes doors that no man can open.

It is important to ask for God's wisdom and revelation to guide us as doors open and close. Remember, however, that it is equally important to ask God to close doors, as it is to ask Him to open them. So many times people focus on praying for God to open doors when some doors may need to be shut before another can open.

---

60 Revelation 3:8

Walking with God is like riding in an elevator. An elevator cannot go anywhere until the doors close. Once those doors close, you have to select a floor, press the button, and presto, you are on your way to the next destination. Then, the doors open, and you are right where you want to be. As we are in the "elevators" of our lives in God, His whispers help us to know what button to press so that the elevator takes us to the place where He desires us to be, and He closes and opens the doors in His timing.

I have seen God's favor revealed time and time again through financial provision and multiplication as well as open and closed doors. Recently, I felt God asking me to let go of a seasonal job that I had had for around five years. It by no means provided for all of my needs, but it did supplement my income when ministry finances became a little lean. Two years ago, I felt like God was whispering to me to let go of this job so that I would be freed up to do the job that He had called me to do. He continued whispering this to me, but I continued to keep this job that had been supplementing my ministry income. In essence, God wanted to free me up to really pursue writing this very book as well as other ministry opportunities, but I wouldn't let go because I was afraid He wouldn't provide. I hovered in this same place for two years until God began to shout instead of whisper. He began saying loud and clear that my little security blanket of a seasonal job had become an idol. Yes...an idol! I trusted in it more than I relied on God, and He was telling me that loud and clear. I told Him I would let go of the job at the end of the month the way one would say "I'll start my diet tomorrow." That felt so wrong, and I knew He was asking more of me. I heard Him gently whisper, "You can continue to provide for yourself through this security blanket you have, or you can trust Me to provide for you." I decided to trust Him, and I left this little job behind.

As I decided to let go of the job, I was shaking. Literally and figuratively. There was this strong temptation to change my mind, but I didn't. I said to some friends of mine, "It's only $250 a month. I know God can provide this. Why am I so worried?"

Two weeks later, a person signed up to be a monthly supporter in the amount of $250! For the two weeks prior to this financial miracle and blessing, it was easy to doubt whether I had heard God, but when I saw His favor in this specific way, not only did it build my faith to trust Him to take care of me but it also showed me that He was backing financially what He had called me to do. In essence, He was multiplying the loaves and fish I brought to Him.

No one likes to experience a closed door and it is especially challenging if God is asking us to be the ones to close the door. Often because we don't have the perspective God has, we become discouraged and frustrated when doors close. It is not until we see another door open and we have the benefit of hindsight, that we become thankful when God closes a door. It is in this that I have come to realize that God's favor is not only in the open door but the closed one as well. We may not always be greeted with immediate results of our obedience, and sometimes confirmations that we heard God's voice correctly will not come until after we obey. However, I have never obeyed and failed to see His favor and presence made manifest in my life. Regardless of whether it's open doors, closed doors, financial provision or a combination of all three, we simply need to follow the favor as we obey God.

Chapter Twenty

Thankfulness

In all of the years of seeing God come through as I have obeyed, I have never wanted to lose my childlike sense of awe of who He is. One of the ways that I preserve this sense of awe of Him is through being thankful and remembering His goodness. When I have seen His provision as I have stepped out to obey His whispers and I see His provision, I want His praise to be on my lips.

I am one who loves a good story, and I value the testimonies God has given me over the years, and the victory they have brought to my life. Revelation 12:11 says, "And they overcame him by the blood of the Lamb, and by the word of their testimony; and they loved not their lives unto the death." The remembered and cherished testimonies we have in God bring victory to us and are catalysts for others to overcome through our stories as well. This is why regularly thanking God and refreshing our memories of His goodness is an important practice in our lives.

In the Old Testament, there was a tremendous sense of importance placed on the actions of remembering God's goodness and having a lifestyle of thankfulness. In fact, thankfulness was so important, that if it was not done, there were consequences. Remember the Israelites who wandered in the wilderness for forty years because of their complaining and failing to remember God? [61]

God called His people to honor feast and holidays that commemorated His provision and admonished the people to pass down the testimonies of God's faithfulness from generation to generation so no one would forget His love and graciousness. One of the most common ways individuals demonstrated this was through building an altar of worship to God in the exact place where God provided. We see Abraham, Noah, Jacob, and others doing this as a way to thank God and remember Him. [62] This is why I make it a practice to do the same by building an "altar" in my heart, recording His provision in my journal, and verbalizing my thanks to God.

This importance of thankfulness and power of thankfulness is also demonstrated in the New Testament. Consider the story of the ten lepers Jesus healed in Luke 17:11-19:

> On the way to Jerusalem he was passing along
> between Samaria and Galilee. And as he entered a
> village, he was met by ten lepers, who stood at a
> distance and lifted up their voices, saying, 'Jesus,

---

[61] Numbers 11:1-3, Numbers 32:13
[62] Genesis 12:6-7, Genesis 8:20-21, Genesis 35:7

Master, have mercy on us.' When he saw them he said to them, 'Go and show yourselves to the priests.' And as they went they were cleansed.[63] Then one of them, when he saw that he was healed, turned back, praising God with a loud voice; and he fell on his face at Jesus' feet, giving him thanks. Now he was a Samaritan. Then Jesus answered, 'Were not ten cleansed? Where are the nine? Was no one found to return and give praise to God except this foreigner?' And he said to him, 'Rise and go your way; your faith has made you well.'[64]

In this passage, only one of the lepers returned to thank Jesus. As a result, he received a great deal more than the other nine lepers. He was not just merely cleansed physically like the other nine, but he was saved, delivered, protected, and made whole. Clearly, there is something very precious that happens when we worship and thank Jesus. There is a divine exchange that occurs, and I believe thankfulness opens us up to more of God's provision in our lives. Thankfulness is something we should give to God simply because He is worthy of it, but there is always extra blessing around the

---

63 The Strong's Greek Dictionary of the New Testament indicates "cleansed" here is the Greek word "katharizo" which means "clean, purge, purify"

64 The Strong's Greek Dictionary of the New Testament indicates "well" here is the Greek word "sozo" which means, "to save, make well or whole, to deliver, protect, heal and preserve."

corner for those who live a life committed to appreciating and thanking God.

Prayer/Call to Action

Below is a prayer you can use to initiate your journey toward recognizing and obeying God's whispers in your life:

Jesus,

I thank you that when you ascended to heaven, You assured us that You would not leave us alone and that You would continue to speak to us through the Comforter, Holy Spirit. I ask that not only would you whisper to me more, but that You would increase my ability to perceive and discern your whispers. I ask for your forgiveness for the times I have not yielded to or obeyed Your voice, and I ask You to help me to obey you from this day forward. I ask You to reveal to me any whispers from the past that I still have the opportunity to obey and give me the steps and strategies that will help me respond to those whispers, and as a result, see You redeem time in my life. I thank you that as I step out to obey what I sense is Your voice, You will be there with favor and multiplication as I bring you my loaves and fish. I thank You that if I am misguided through a misinterpretation of Your voice, You will redirect my path and reset my footing. I choose to trust You, and with Your help, Your voice instead of the voice of fear will set the course of my life. According to John 10:27,"Your sheep hear Your voice and another's they will not follow," so I ask for Your voice to be my guide and for Your wisdom and counsel to surround me and empower me to obey your voice. I thank you that when I ask You for bread, You will not give me a stone, and as I ask for Your whispers today, You will be faithful to speak to me. "Now to Him Who is able to do far more than I could ever imagine....to Him be the glory!"

Amen

I would love to continue to be a part of your journey with God, and, just as I have shared my stories with you, I would love to hear your stories as you step out in obedience. Please share your journeys with me and give me the blessing of hearing how God's whispers have come alive in your story. Please visit www.tarabrowder.com for more information on my ministry, speaking itinerary, contact information, and other media available from Tara Browder Media.

Many Blessings!

Tara

Also from Tara Browder Media:

Some of the greatest longings of the soul are to be wanted, desired, and chosen. We all want to be to be somebody's somebody, but can the fulfillment of this desire for identity and belonging ever be *fully* realized in the context of romance or relationships? I had always heard that God was supposed to be the one responsible for completely meeting these desires, but, honestly, I had a difficult time knowing how to practically get to that place with Him. In fact, I often wondered if it was even possible to achieve this kind of rest for the soul outside the realm of romance. *Overcoming Bride* chronicles my story of a beautiful journey toward marriage that suffered an abrupt detour. As a result, one of my greatest quests began---the fight to find God, identity, and belonging in the shadows of shocking loss.

24769491R00082

Made in the USA
Middletown, DE
05 October 2015